EXCHANGE NETWORKS
AND COMMUNITY POLITICS

Volume 75, Sage Library of Social Research

Sage Library of Social Research

Exchange Networks and Community Politics

Joseph Galaskiewicz

Preface by Herman Turk

Volume 75
SAGE LIBRARY OF
SOCIAL RESEARCH

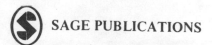 SAGE PUBLICATIONS   Beverly Hills   London

Copyright © 1979 by Sage Publications, Inc.

For information address:

SAGE PUBLICATIONS, INC.
275 South Beverly Drive
Beverly Hills, California 90212

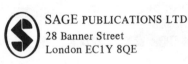

SAGE PUBLICATIONS LTD
28 Banner Street
London EC1Y 8QE

Printed in the United States of America

Library of Congress Cataloging in Publication Data

Galaskiewicz, Joseph.
    Exchange Networks and Community Politics
    (Sage library of social research; v. 75)
    Bibliography: p. 195
    1. Community organization. 2. Community organiza-
tion—Case studies. 3. Interoreganizational relations.
4. Decision-making, Group—Case studies. 5. Power
(Social sciences)—Case studies. I. Title.
HM131.G23   301.18'32   78-21008
ISBN 0-8039-1137-8
ISBN 0-8039-1138-6 pbk.

FIRST PRINTING

CONTENTS

ACKNOWLEDGMENTS

I am a firm believer in the principle that knowledge is cumulative. There are no such things as new ideas, just syntheses of old ones mixed in with a little practical experience. My own experience with community organization began during my undergraduate days at Loyola University of Chicago. During the summer months I worked as a community organizer for the city of Chicago's Department of Human Resources trying, with mixed success, to set up interorganizational "systems" of my own. In my graduate work at the University of Chicago I was encouraged by Morris Janowitz to do my master's thesis on the DHR, and following that I became involved in a study of interorganizational networks on Chicago's southwest side with Irving Spergel. My work with Professors Janowitz and Spergel gave me invaluable experience and motivated me to do further research on the structure of community institutions.

In 1973 I was fortunate enough to take a seminar on Social Network Analysis from Edward Laumann who was a visiting professor at the University of Chicago at that time. My own interest in community interorganizational networks converged with his interest in general systems analysis. When he came to the University of Chicago the following Fall Quarter, we agreed that I would replicate his study of German community elites in two northern Illinois communities in exchange for the opportunity to do my dissertation on the interorganizational networks in one of the communities, Towertown. Needless to say, without Professor Laumann's support this monograph would never have been possi-

7

ble. Both Mr. Laumann and Peter Marsden, who worked as a research assistant with me in graduate school, have given freely of their time and have been most generous in making comments on the number of revisions that the manuscript has gone through.

Others in the sociology department at the University of Chicago also have been of great inspiration to me. The influence of James Coleman is apparent throughout the monograph but especially in my development of a purposive action perspective. Terry Clark has also been a great help throughout the years. My fellow graduate students, Jim Lynch, Carol Heimer, Lynn Pettler, and Marge Troha, not only assisted me in collecting and organizing the data but were valuable sources of criticism and ideas throughout the research. It is rare to find such stimulating company.

With my move to the University of Minnesota, I developed a new set of colleagues who have been equally helpful. Don Martindale, Rhoda Estep, Bob Leik, Ray Bradley, and Barbara Rauschenbach have read parts of the monograph and have given me useful feedback. Mark Mongiat has been an invaluable research assistant. Herman Turk at the University of Southern California has also been very supportive during my stay at Minnesota.

When research runs over a number of years, there are usually several different institutions that help to support the project. The costs of gathering and organizing the data were paid for by a NSF research grant to Professor Laumann (SOC73-13113). Funds for data analysis were provided by the University of Chicago, Loyola University of Chicago, and the University of Minnesota. During this last year, a NIMH Small Grant (1RO3 MH29511) supported a research assistant for this monograph and other research related to the Towertown study. During the summer of 1977, the Graduate School of the University of Minnesota awarded me a research grant so that I could finish writing the manuscript. Money for secretarial help has come from a variety of sources, but the bulk of the cost of typing the manuscript has been absorbed by the Department of Sociology at the University of Minnesota. A special thanks to Don MacTavish for this assistance.

Although many individuals have helped me in preparing this monograph, its content, of course, is ultimately my responsibility.

Traditionally the author attributes the strengths of the monograph to the help and insight of others, while taking the blame for any shortcomings himself. In this case I can see no reason to break with tradition.

University of Minnesota   *Joseph Galaskiewicz*
July 1978

PREFACE

Graphing the social networks of a community is not new, nor is the view that relations among organizations are important to its life. Also, previous dissertations have extended mainstream method and content to a degree that merited their publication, virtually intact.

Yet Joseph Galaskiewicz's portrayal of Towertown is new because it combines all three of these features. His reverence for data—evident from their collection through their analysis—echoes the painstaking creation of community sociograms more than forty years ago. But the similarity ends right there. Simple diagrams of friendship choices based on socioeconomic status have given way, first of all, to multidimensional mapping by computer over a variety of contents. Second, the empirical emphases have been deflected, in part, from links among persons and families in the small community to connections among organizations throughout an entire city. Galaskiewicz has provided benchmarks along these lines.

His strategy is to group formal organizations with one another according to path distances based on dyadic links involving money, information, and sociopolitical support. The map produced by each of these three symbolic media is used to identify such topological attributes as proximity and centrality, whose association with various characteristics of organizations and of organizational pairs is assessed. He is also able to identify relationships between these topological constructs and such traditional concerns of community research as participation in local issues, reputational influence, and consensus among elites.

Galaskiewicz refers to a variety of community imageries. In being far-ranging, he risks unwarranted attacks for lacks of closure, parsimony, or deductive rigor. However, he has risen above these eventualities by showing that his research strategy can ground various theoretical perspectives, not just his own. For example, although he appears to have favored a utilitarian framework, he is able to point to findings that suggest its confounding by solidarities and ideological similarities. That his methodology is capable of generating isomorphisms between data and prevalent models is a very important point.

There are alternative procedures for describing networks in detail, but they have not been tried in the community. For example, organizational actors can be clustered on the basis of similarity of connections rather than proximity. Or "atoms" larger than dyads might be employed. Establishing the relative merits of these alternatives for community research, however, requires their application. Their application, in turn, can profit from the lessons that are reported in this book.

Joseph Galaskiewicz provides in these pages an important methodological contribution to case study of the small city. He has demonstrated its worth through a prodigious one-person effort. In so doing, he has laid bare procedures, empirical descriptions, and even his thought processes in such detail that one can benefit in a variety of ways: From evaluating the strengths and weaknesses of network analysis, through speculating about the odd regression coefficient, to considering the possibilities he suggests for comparative urban research. In adapting his methods to the details of interorganizational networks, he has produced a work that both serves as a model and as a spur to do more.

Herman Turk
University of Southern California

Chapter 1

SOCIAL ACTORS AND SOCIAL STRUCTURE

The study of social structure and social choice is of central importance to sociological inquiry. Rightly or wrongly, structure and choice are often pitted against one another. The "needs" of the society confront the "needs" of the individual, and some sort of adaptation on the part of the individual or the structure becomes necessary. Usually the process of adaptation does not go smoothly. Institutionalized relationships are often difficult to change because of their complexity and the vested interests which they support, and individuals often become frustrated with those structures which supposedly exist to serve their needs and do not. The response on the part of individuals may be either outright rebellion, the establishment of alternative institutions, or acquiescence; from the structure we might expect repression or minor structural change. Most of the time it is a little of each.

Although these "conflict" situations are important as they usually introduce some sort of social change into the system, the interaction between individual social choice and macrosocial structures has not received the attention it deserves in the sociological literature. The early work of Merton (Stinchcombe, 1975) and Parsons (1951) and, more recently, the work of Hernes (1976) and Coleman (1973a) have addressed this issue. More typically, sociologists have opted either to explore the abstract configurations of macrostructure (e.g., Parsons; Lipset) or to examine the behavior of "rational actors" engaging in ad hoc coalition or exchange relationships on a microlevel, e.g., Homans; Coleman (Blau, 1975).

It is my hope in this monograph to extend theory and research which seeks to understand more fully the tensions and conflicts between social structures and individual self-interests. Although the empirical research is on behavior of formal organizations in a medium-size midwestern community, we hope that the reader may gain some insight into how social structures and individuals' interests can be analyzed in general. Furthermore, from this study of collective decision making, I hope that the reader may also see how these special types of conflict are reconciled.

Social Structure: What's the Fuss All About?

Traditionally, a social structure is characterized as a persisting pattern of social relationships among social positions. This conceptualization of structure is used both by Laumann (1966, 1973) and implicitly by Blau (1977) and borrows from the work of Parsons (1951). Supposedly these positions and the relations between them evolve over time in response to conditions in the society and exist independent of the particular incumbents. The structure is institutionalized as roles are defined for the different positions. Once institutionalized, actors can move in and out of these positions as they take on or shed roles. Through a process of socialization individuals learn the rights and privileges as well as the responsibilities and hardships attached to the positions. Ultimately the social structure, which includes both the positions and the relationships between positions, is given meaning in the context of collective values which, in turn, confer legitimacy upon it.

There is little doubt that individuals still aspire to institutionalized status positions, invest enormous amounts of resources in education and training to attain these positions, and once these positions are achieved, perform their tasks and duties faithfully. There is, however, a growing consensus among sociologists that this concept of social structure is just not adequate for studying the behavior of different types of social actors. The behavior of corporate actors, for example, cannot be explained in reference to the roles that these actors assume. In fact, these organizations were originally established precisely to avoid the cultural constraints that surrounded "natural persons." Although large corporate actors are bound by laws which prohibit or mandate some relational patterns, corporate actors, for the most part, are free from almost all other normative constraints (Coleman, 1974).

An alternative model of social structure views it as an emergent phenomenon. Nadel (1957) argues that to arrive at the social structure of a group, we ought to abstract from a population of actors general networks of relationships. Positions in the social structure (i.e., network) "emerge" from the interaction one observes. The recent work of Harrison White and his associates (Lorrain and White, 1971; White, Boorman, and Breiger, 1976; Boorman and White, 1976; Breiger, Boorman, and Arabie, 1975) and of Ronald Burt (Burt, 1976; Burt, 1977a, 1977b) demonstrate empirically how this type of structural analysis might be done using the mathematical principle of structural equivalence. Roles in the system are then inferred looking at the configuration of positions and the relationships between them.

The work of Paul Holland and his associates (Holland and Leinhardt, 1977, 1978; Wasserman, 1977) also view social structure as an emergent phenomenon, but from a slightly different perspective. Their focus is on the identification of certain structural properties within a network that explain the distribution of relationships within the set of nodes. These properties are viewed as "laws" which give direction to the evolution of group structure over time. The Holland-Leinhardt-Wasserman models could build on the work of White, Breiger, Boorman, and Burt by taking the positions identified through hierarchical clustering algorithms as their nodes and model structural change based on the relationships between the positions. Regardless, social structure is seen as an emergent phenomenon which operates independent of a cultural system. Although Holland and his associates do not discuss social roles, one can infer that macrorole structures and social values play a minimal role in the actual development of their relational systems.

The conceptualization of social structure used in this study borrows from both traditions, while having unique features of its own. We will define a social structure as a persisting pattern of influence relations which exists among a set of social actors in a social organization. The structure of the group is both a cultural and emergent phenomenon, but in ways that are much different from those articulated in the perspectives just discussed. We will argue that social structures emerge out of the purposive action of social actors (whether they be individuals or organizations) who seek to realize their self-interests and, depending on their ability and interests, will negotiate routinized patterns of relationships that enhance these interests. At the same time, the way in which particular resource networks will be routinized will be determined by the functional needs that the medium of exchange serves in the social organization. In the sections below we will develop both these theses in more detail.

PURPOSIVE ACTION AND EMERGENT SOCIAL STRUCTURE

Viewing social structures as emerging out of the pursuit of self-interest draws us to exchange theory and models of purposive action. These theoretical frameworks see each actor in a social organization as a rational bargaining agent with a set of interests and resources which he seeks to protect or enhance. The assumptions regarding social interaction are similar to those made with regard to microeconomic behavior (Coleman, 1966; Downs, 1957) and game situations (Luce and Raiffa, 1957; von Neumann and Morgenstern, 1947). The only constraints governing interaction are antithetical norms of reciprocity and power dependency. Under the former, actors are expected to play fairly with one another exchanging goods and services which are comparable in value (Gouldner, 1960; Homans, 1958); while under the latter, actors are expected to maximize their autonomy while making others dependent on them (Emerson, 1962).[1]

Many social scientists have been able to develop models which are based on individual pursuit of self-interest, but few have focused on the aggregated networks of influence relationships that this gives rise to (for an exception, see Banfield, 1961). Structurally, the whole is not greater than the sum of its parts; however, the configuration of influence relationships can be described or analyzed as a social fact in and of itself. Although social structures are constructed through individual social choice processes on the microlevel, our thesis is that they exist as powerful influences themselves delimiting options in the social organization on the macrolevel (see Hernes, 1976). Marsden and Laumann (1977) discuss this issue at length and point out the dangers that await researchers who seek to analyze, for example, coalition formation without being aware of the existing structural ties between actors.

If emergent social structures are to be explained in terms of the interests and resources of the actors in the system, then it follows that social stability and social change will also be explained by looking at the characteristics of actors. Stability is rooted in the interests of certain actors to maintain structural arrangements in order to protect their own positions of power. On the other hand, social change is rooted in the interests of less powerful social actors to displace those in dominant positions and put themselves in these positions instead.

There is a number of advantages to viewing social stability from this perspective. Functional theories commonly project teleological ends and/or equilibrium states onto social systems (e.g., Parsons, 1951; Buckley, 1968; Deutsch, 1963; Hawley, 1951). We believe that such assumptions are unreasonable (Martindale, 1965), and we would add that they are also unnecessary to explain stability in the social order. Rather than thinking of the social system in cybernetic or organismic terms, our position is that social structures persist in order to maintain the power differentials among actors in the social order, which, in turn, increase the life opportunities of some actors while reducing the opportunities of others (Stinchcombe, 1968; Dahrendorf, 1958; Alford, 1975).

Therefore, it is not difficult to understand why social structures are often seen as conservative forces in a social order. The hierarchy of established influence relationships defines the probability that any one actor can influence another. As it becomes clear to an actor that his chances of being influential are limited, he is less likely to take the initiative to change the social order (Blalock, 1967; Dahl, 1961; Clark, 1968). Furthermore, if ideologies emerge to legitimate the modus operandi and camouflage the power of dominants, subordinates will be distracted and will not recognize the disadvantageous position that they are in in the social structure (see Bachrach and Baratz, 1962, 1963; Lasswell, 1936; Alford, 1975).

These arguments almost smack of a crude Marxism, since the social structures of society are said to reflect the interests of dominant or ruling elites. Although Marxists would find our theory entertaining (but not compatible with their own), so would a number of non-Marxists. For example, Michels's (1949) study of oligarchical structures, Hunter's (1953) description of community power structures, and Rakove's (1976) analysis of big city political machines all make the argument that large scale structural forms emerge and persist in order to maintain and enhance the interests of certain actors. Ideologies or belief systems may be used to legitimate existing structural patterns, yet the network of dependency relations (and subsequent obligations) is the critical factor which defines the structure.

To argue that structures persist and that ideologies evolve over time to maintain them is not to preclude social change. In contrast to Parsons (1951), whose focus is on the socialization of actors into existing social institutions, we would emphasize that actors have the capacity to transcend their institutional environments and engage in purposive action that can effectively change social structures (Chapin, 1928; Martindale, 1962).[2] Although this may sound naive, we feel that it is a point of view that should be given more attention.

As the persistence of social structures can be traced to the interests of actors to retain their positions of power in a social organization, change can be traced to the interests of actors to increase their power.[3] By liberating themselves of the need for resources which others control, by securing resources which others need, by finding alternative suppliers of resources, or by using coercion, subordinates can initiate action which could result in the displacement of dominant actors (Emerson, 1962). An example of this process is found in Dahl's study of New Haven politics, where the distribution of power was changed radically by historical changes which altered the distribution of resources among interest groups. As actors accrued resources, new coalitions were possible, and the structure of influence relations was subject to change. Indeed, we expect that actors who have power in the system will react to challengers and that the "power structure" may be too tightly organized to allow for change. However, we still expect that change will come primarily from the ranks of subordinates who seek a redistribution of power in the system.

We might note that our perspective puts us somewhat at odds with traditional social action theory and pluralism as well. Rather than viewing innovators, intellectuals, and revolutionaries as "prophets" of a new age or world order, our perspective is much more cynical (Martindale, 1962). We view change agents simply as actors who are interested in amassing as much power as they possibly can and will use whatever means available to gain the advantage they seek. We also part ways with the pluralist (e.g., Polsby, 1963; Truman, 1951; and Rose, 1967), since we hold that the very "rules of the game" and the institutions established to govern the competition among interest groups are ideological forms that work for or against the interests of different actors. Furthermore, we do not view the system as necessarily being "in balance" if social structural forms persist over time. Our model makes no assumption that order is a function of a mutual trade off between equals, rather we view structural stability as a temporary state based on inequalities which prevent subordinates from challenging the legitimacy of dominant elites (Wilson, 1973).

FUNCTIONAL DIFFERENCES AMONG SOCIAL STRUCTURES

While we argued that social structures arise out of the purposive action of self-interested actors, we also argued that the particular medium or resource through which actors interact will affect the way in which social structures take shape. To date there has been very little research on how the content of social interaction affects the way networks are formed. Research has described multiplex networks; however, typically relationships have been simply aggregated (e.g., White, Boorman, and Breiger, 1976; Knoke and Rogers, 1978; Burt, 1977a, 1977b). It is very discouraging that there is virtually no systematic research on the properties of different types of resource exchange systems themselves.[4]

The approach we offer is to identify certain needs that actors try to satisfy through interaction and the respective resources (or media of exchange) which facilitate this need fulfillment. As there are different purposes in social interaction, different patterns should emerge within different resource networks. Although we could identify several different types of resources relevant to different needs of actors, we choose to study only three. We will assume that exchanges of money are relevant to actors' satisfying their adaptive needs, exchanges of information are relevant to meeting problem solving needs of actors, and exchanges of moral support are relevant to satisfying legitimacy needs. We realize that we are, in effect, projecting meanings onto interaction which may be at odds with the particular meanings which the actors themselves have. However, our goal is to identify generic types of relationships that have a general relevance to actors, and our strategy seems to us to be the best available.

One basic need of actors is to secure goods and services from the environment (Parsons, 1966). Especially in a highly differentiated social system, actors are dependent upon others for the raw materials to maintain their own productive capacity. Money is one institutionalized medium of exchange which permits the ready acquisition of facilities for goal attainment and, for certain actors, serves as a mechanism regulating the distribution of outputs (see Parsons and Smelser, 1956; Aldrich, 1975; and Benson, 1975).

Actors also need criteria upon which to make strategic decisions regarding the allocation of their resources. This need is met primarily through exchanges of information with others in the environment. Information about general environmental developments and the activities of other actors reduces uncertainty for actors, helps actors to readjust goals, and gives direction to the use of resources. Furthermore, information exchanges may serve as the basis for the generation of trust among actors in a system; such trust seems to be essential for the establishment of joint problem-solving efforts (Kornblum, 1974; Coleman, 1971).

Finally, actors must be able to legitimate their actions and policies to one another (see Parsons, 1966). In order to avoid negative sanctions from others, actors must be seen as pursuing interests which somehow contribute to the collective good. We would argue that exchanges of moral support among actors in the environment would help to establish and maintain actors' legitimacy in a social organization. In a sense, then, these exchanges give moral meaning to actors' behavior. Needless to say, some actors elicit more support (i.e., legitimacy) than others; however, some level of legitimacy and support is required by any actor which seeks to participate fully in the life of the collectivity.[5]

In sum, we argue that actors enter into relationships with other actors through the exchange of certain resources which help them to meet certain of their functional needs. Needless to say, the three resources that we will examine are not the only resources relevant to the adaptive, problem solving, and legitimacy needs of actors as many others are as well; nevertheless, in this monograph we will focus exclusively on these three.

Although the meaning of these resource exchanges may be traced to the functional needs of individual actors, we must remind ourselves that we are primarily interested in the aggregation of these dyadic exchanges into community-wide networks. From here on these resource networks will be referred to as institutional networks.

We are not the first to suggest that the relational components (as opposed to the normative components) of social institutions be "operationalized" by looking at selected social networks among actors in a community. Mitchell (1969) approached the study of social institutions in a similar way:

> Institutional analysis involves abstraction of a specified type of content from the links in a network of multiplex relationships in real life, and the representation of these relationships in systematic and summary

form. The sequence of abstraction, after the initial act of observation, is from actual behaviors to multiplex linkages in networks, from multiplex relationships to what Barnes calls "partial networks," that is in terms of a single specified content, and from partial networks to the institutional structures (1969:45).

By "abstraction" one can identify adaptive networks based on the flows of money, decision-making networks based on the flow of information (e.g., Laumann and Pappi, 1976), and solidarity networks based on the flow of moral support (see also Srinivas and Beteille, 1964).

Social Status in Social Organizations

So far we have discussed how social structure will emerge out of the purposive action of actors and will probably take a form which reflects the functional significance of the resources being exchanged. We have not, however, discussed position in social structures and how we might go about identifying an actor's status in a social organization using a network perspective.

Traditionally an actor's "status" in a social organization is rooted in the cultural order. Roles specify the contributions which different social positions make to the survival of the social system and the benefits which incumbents should enjoy. Very simply, the more critical a position, the more "status" it should have and the more its incumbents should be rewarded. Although this argument has a long history in functional thought (see Parsons, 1951; Davis and Moore, 1945; Keller, 1963), it is now experiencing a rebirth in ecological theory (e.g., Hannan and Freeman, 1977; Lincoln, 1977; Hawley, 1963). Although the current version speaks less of stratification, the implication is that units which are effective boundary spanning functionairies occupy a key position in the structure and consequently will and should be rewarded accordingly.

We mentioned that those who view social structures as emergent phenomena (see, e.g., Nadel, 1957) also have a clearly defined notion of what constitutes a structural position. Actors occupy a particular position in a social structure to the extent that their relations with other actors in the social organization are similar. Following Nadel (1957), positions in a social order are identified by examining the interaction profiles of actors in a number of different relational contexts. Actors are grouped into subsets based on the distribution of "zero blocks" or "empty spaces" in their total interaction pattern. Consequently, members of the same status group or block are actors who have a similar profile of null relationships. In many ways this approach to the identification of status positions parallels Merton's (1957a) discussion of role sets. Hierarchy among positions is then determined by looking at the "density" of relationships between positions. Several very interesting strategies have been developed that can summarize very complex interrelational patterns (Breiger and Pattison, 1978; Burt, 1977a, 1977b; Allen, 1978), and efforts are now being made to draw comparisons between different types of relational systems (Boorman and White, 1976).

In this paper we will focus on a somewhat different type of "position" that actors occupy in social networks—their relative centrality. Furthermore, we expect that an actor's status (i.e., his power) will be a function of his centrality. We want to caution the reader immediately that we do not necessarily equate being central with having a "high" status and being peripheral with having a "low" status. Whether occupying a central position in a relational system will enable an actor to "get his way" more often than not is an empirical question. One could argue that an actor who is more autonomous (i.e., peripheral) would be more powerful since he would be more self-sufficient. Nevertheless, by identifying how central an actor is, we have given him a "place" in a network structure.

In analyzing power and social status in relational systems, many sociologists have focused on centrality (e.g., Rogers, 1974; Harary, Norman, and Cartwright, 1965; Bavelas, 1960; Benson, 1975; Cook, 1977; Laumann and Pappi, 1976). Centrality in a social influence network has been identified as a general structural position which has definite structural properties of its own (Shils, 1975). An actor in the center of a system of relationships is at a minimal social distance to all other actors. Therefore, the "centrality" of an actor tells us how dependent or independent actors are on others in the social organization. Actors in the center of a network have many different direct and indirect inflows and outflows and thus are highly interdependent; those on the periphery of a network are less involved in interaction by definition and thus more autonomous. In a sense, we are positioning actors in the relational system by ascertaining how "dense" their relational sets are.

Problems of Collective Decision-Making

So far we have simply outlined our ideas on social structure, noting how our treatment of structure and status differs from that of other students. In this section we want to go back and consider in a little more detail the interaction between individual actors, who seek power and have their own functional needs to satisfy, and those emergent phenomena that we have characterized as community institutional structures. We will examine this interaction in the context of a very simple question: what happens in a social organization when individual actors have to act as a unit and solve collective problems.

The answer is not immediately obvious, for it would be very difficult to generate any collective action in a social organization where all actors are autonomous and each has his own set of interests. Although purposive action models can explain how different actors "make deals" among themselves and settle their accounts with one another (e.g., Arrow, 1955; Coleman, 1966; Niemi and Weisberg, 1972), they are incapable of explaining how social organizations which have functional problems of their own are able to aggregate energies of private interests to respond to these problems (see Olson, 1965).

In sociology an interest in comparative social organizational analysis and, in particular, comparative community research has kept this issue alive (Hawley, 1963; Clark, 1971; Aiken and Alford, 1970; Turk, 1970, 1973a, 1973b, 1977; Lincoln, 1976; and Smith, 1976). Typically, input-throughput-output models have tried to determine the effects of both demographic as well as organizational and interorganizational structures on system-level policy outputs. Unfortunately, most measures of the "community decision-making structure" have been quite crude and difficult to interpret theoretically (see Laumann, Galaskiewicz, and Marsden, 1978). Furthermore, theories which could explain patterns of interest group conflict on the microlevel were mute on the matter of generating collective power on the macrolevel (e.g., Dahl), while systems theories of collective action developed on the macrolevel were silent on how different interest groups reconciled their differences on the microlevel (e.g., Hawley, Turk). In other works, while the literature has recognized that there are two types of "power" being exercised in a community (individual actors' power and collective power), it has not been able to show how one influence process influences the other.

The purpose of this section is to review how other theorists have tried to explain how collective action is possible in a social organization. Once we have critiqued them, we will then offer our own answer to the question. We will argue that the solution to the dilemma lies in the interplay between individual actors and the emergent institutional structures that currently exist in the social organization.

TRUST AND THE GENERATION OF COLLECTIVE POWER

One way to generate collective power is to solicit resources from actors in the social organization and to designate agents to use these resources as they see fit on behalf of the collectivity. In other words, if members of a collectivity can convince one another to relinquish control over their own resources and put that control in the hands of collective agents, the collectivity will have enough resources or credit to act in its environment. Obviously this manner of generating power in a collectivity can last only so long as the actors have confidence or trust in the collective agents.

Theorists have suggested two different bases upon which this confidence might rest. On the one hand, Parsons (1963) suggests that the willingness of actors to relinquish control over their own resources is based on common values that members share. To the extent that collective agents are seen as legitimate and acting in accord with dominant values, actors will forfeit control over their own resources to collective agents trusting that the resources will be used for the purpose of achieving collective goals.

On the other hand, Gamson (1968) would argue that actors would forfeit control over their resources, only if they believed or trusted that collective agents would somehow be able to utilize their resources to reap a greater benefit for them. In this case, trust in collective agents is based on a rational cost/benefit calculus which evaluates the probability of realizing a return for one's investment of resources. This conceptualization of trust and collective power is quite similar to Coleman's description of how actors contribute and become committed to corporate actors (Coleman, 1973a). An interesting point in Coleman's discussion is his argument that though benefits may be quite enticing, the power of corporate actors relative to the power of individuals who invest in it becomes much, much greater.

POWER DEPENDENCY AND COLLECTIVE POWER

Another way to generate collective power is through the institutionalization of dependency relations. According to power dependency theory, an actor has power over another actor to the extent that the first actor possesses something which the second actor wants and the second actor's options for obtaining that object elsewhere are limited (see Emerson, 1962; Benson, 1975; Aldrich and Pfeffer, 1976). In this situation the second actor is obliged or dependent upon the first actor and thus the first actor can exercise influence over him. This theory, of course, is based on the assumption that actors agree that relationships ought to be balanced, reciprocal, or equitable.

Blau (1964) went beyond earlier theorists in explaining how resource dependency could be institutionalized and transformed into a mechanism to generate and maintain collective power. As dependency ties remain stable, norms develop that rationalize the power differential between those who occupy dominant positions and those who occupy subordinate positions. The important point of Blau's theory is that collective power is not based on the trust or good will of members in the collectivity, but on the ideology that subordinate actors owe deference to dominant actors who, in turn, act on behalf of the collectivity.

DISCUSSION

It is clear that all these theories are developed from an interactionist perspective. The distinguishing characteristic of the first, however, is that collective power is based on trust in collective agents. In the second, ideology and power dependency is more critical. Parsons, Gamson, and Coleman view collective agents as a "holding company" which receives resources from individual social actors and aggregates them for collective purposes. There is, however, one serious problem with this approach. It assumes that for collective power to exist there must be a set of actors which recruits and aggregates resources from member actors. If we accept this, then we can only think of this set of "agents" either as an alter ego of all individual actors in the collectivity, or we must resign ourselves to the fact that so-called "collective" agents constitute an interest group themselves which seeks to aggregate and monopolize power for its own benefit in the name of the collective good (see Gamson, 1968; Dahrendorf, 1959). We must reject the first conclusion on logical grounds and the second on the grounds that one really has not generated collective power at all.

On the other hand, Emerson and Blau view collective power as something generated out of the institutionalized "stand off" between dominant and subordinate actors. In this case a monopoly over resources generates the condition where one set of actors (supposedly an elite acting in the "collective interests") is able to exercise its options over less resourceful actors, because of the latter's dependency on it. But this also seems problematic. One of the basic premises of this model is that collective power is possible only if the options of a subset of actors are restricted. This stipulation precludes any generation of power under conditions of equity or voluntary action. If options increase and actors maxi-

mize their autonomy from one another, the structural prerequi-
sites for collective action are simply not available.

In light of our discussion we must reject both theoretical
perspectives. While the first set of theories necessitates the generation of a set of collective agents and subsequently the creation of
an elite in the social organization, the second precludes collective
action under voluntary or egalitarian conditions.

A RESOURCE NETWORK MODEL OF COLLECTIVE POWER

In developing a comprehensive theory of social power, we must
take two things into account. First, within a social organization
individual actors will pursue their self-interests establishing and
terminating social relationships as their own needs vary; and,
second, the social organization itself must have a capacity to act as
a collectivity to respond to changes in its environments and meet
its functional needs. We will argue that to incorporate both in a
theory of collective power, we ought to focus on how decisions
made at the individual actor level generate social structures in the
social organization which, in turn, affect the way that actors
respond to contingencies which threaten them as a collectivity
(Aldrich and Pfeffer, 1976; Laumann, Galaskiewicz, and Marsden,
1978; and Hernes, 1976).

On the individual level we view social structures as the product
of different actors striving to maximize their own self-interests,
setting up interaction networks to secure needed resources from
one another, and increasing their influence over others. To this
point, our thinking is similar to the traditional microtheories of
purposive action outlined above.

However, once all dyadic transactions have been routinized,
there then exists a network structure that actors must take into
account before they can take any subsequent action. For example,
before actors i and j can establish a new relationship between
themselves, they must take into account their relationships to all
actors k and assess how their proposed interaction will affect the
status of their current set of relations to k. For example, Evan
(1966), Warren (1967), and Perrow (1970:121-130) discuss how

the interorganizational field, once established, limits and shapes individual organizations' subsequent interorganizational behavior. The structure, in effect, binds the actor into a set of social obligations. Law, tradition, or an ideology of cooperation as well as norms of reciprocity are effective mechanisms that hold actors to their commitments. Furthermore, once structural relationships among actors are set, we would argue that the sheer complexity of dependency and influence patterns will discourage further relational jockeying among actors.

But if a set of actors does need to act as a collectivity, we also expect that this infrastructure of social relations will provide a ready means by which actors in the social organization can generate an effective collective response. Because there exists a hierarchy of influence relations already, certain actors who occupy "more dense" (i.e., more central) positions in the network are likely candidates to be recruited to leadership roles. To begin with, an actor who occupies a more dominant position in a resource exchange network obviously has a great interest in maintaining that network. Thus, there will be a greater willingness to take on a leadership role if that particular resource network is threatened in any way. In addition, the opportunity to assume leadership in a crisis may provide an actor some extra "credit" that can be readily cashed in after the crisis is over. But actors who are more peripheral are also likely to want central actors to assume leadership roles. Actors in the center of the system are "natural" leaders since they have a greater capacity to mobilize actors in the collectivity. Their minimal social distance to others in the system would be an asset in establishing problem-solving coalitions. Furthermore, more peripheral actors do have a certain recourse if leaders betray them. An actor's status rests on his relationships with others in the system and not on his individual resources. Consequently, more peripheral actors can undermine an actor's position by avoiding him or discriminating against him in their everyday interaction.

We must remember, however, that if dominant actors exercise power on behalf of the collectivity, it is based neither on their formal authority nor the trust that others have in them. Actors in more central positions assume leadership because they have a special interest in resolving the conflict in order to maintain their own power in the community. In addition, they control a special resource for conflict resolution—the potential to draw other actors into a problem-solving coalition. A final reason is that they can be held accountable by others, who, if disgruntled, might undermine their position in the social structure. Our theory, then, suggests that collective power is really nothing more than the exercise of private power on behalf of collective interests. It is not that new leadership roles are created in crisis situations; it is just that certain actors with certain relational assets are selected by others in the social organization to act on behalf of the collectivity. In a way their "private" actions are simply redefined as "collective" action by others in the group.

Numerous examples of this process can be found in the decision-making literature. For example, Banfield (1961) and Perrucci and Pilisuk (1970) demonstrated how interorganizational network structures create certain niches or positions that help certain actors become much more important than others in decision-making situations. Certain actors can much more easily mobilize resources and put together coalitions because they are "interorganizational leaders" or because others owe them debts from previous transactions. In either case it is their relational position in the network that determines their role in community decision-making. Although "structural positions" per se are not analyzed in these studies, it is apparent that actors in certain positions are not free to build alliances that violate ongoing structural relationships. Rather they have to follow strategies that are sensitive to their respective positions in the community interorganizational networks.

So What Else is New?

Before we go on, we should stop to consider just how our approach to the study of social structure and our theory of collective decision-making attempt to integrate several different theoretical traditions. We will argue that our theory differs from more traditional sociological theories of social organization in that it borrows both from interactionist theory and functional theory in its attempt to explain the generation of collective power.

On the one hand, we borrow from the behavioralist or interactionist perspective insofar as we focus on the fates and fortunes of individual actors. We assume that social actors have certain goals and that they will act in a purposive manner in order to accomplish these goals. A common strategy will be to establish exchange/dependency relations with others in the social organization. Motives of actors will be primarily selfish with rare acts of altruism.

On the other hand, we borrow from functionalist theory. We state quite clearly that individual actors have certain needs. Furthermore, we argue that certain symbolic media of exchange or resources are institutionalized in order to enable actors in the social organization to satisfy these different needs. The media we identified were money, information, and moral support. Supposedly these media help to meet the economic, problem-solving, and legitimacy needs of actors in the social order by facilitating interaction relevant to the satisfaction of these needs.

Although we borrow from both traditions, our definitions and theory differ in many ways from traditional interactionist theory and functional theory. For example, whereas most interaction theory is formulated in strictly social psychological terms, we argue that actors are motivated to increase their power *and* to satisfy certain functional needs that all actors must satisfy. Furthermore, we lay heavy emphasis on the fact that dyadic relations give rise to complex macrostructures which, in turn, shape the course of collective action.

We also make several departures from traditional functional analysis. We make no a priori assumption that the social organization must return to a state of equilibrium or that it was ever in such a state to begin with. Also, there is no discussion of social values or their overriding importance in shaping structural patterns. More importantly, our approach can handle social conflict among interest groups and can actually use this conflict to help explain the emergence of institutional networks and the generation of collective power.

By combining elements of both behaviorist theory and functionalist theory we have hopefully made some progress in bridging the gap between micro- and macro-levels of social organization analysis. The main advantage to our perspective is that it is not an "either-or" approach to the study of power. We can study both the fortunes of different actors as they struggle to dominate resource network structures as well as the effect of aggregate network patterns on problem-solving in the collectivity.

The Study of a "Real Life" System

This monograph will take our general theoretical approach as outlined above and apply it to the study of one type of social organization, the community. Although this social organization has been researched over and over again, we feel that our perspective will shed new light on some old and yet not fully understood issues. In particular, we will focus on the formal organization as the key actor in this social organization and examine its behavior with respect to other community corporate actors and the local environment. A number of researchers have pointed out the primacy of formal organizations in the modern community (see Coleman, 1957; Banfield, 1961; Turk, 1969, 1973a, 1973b, 1977; Perrucci and Pilisuk, 1970; Aiken and Alford, 1970; Spergel, 1976; Kaufmann, 1959; and Warren, Rose, and Bergunder, 1974).

Compared to other types of actors in the community, we feel safe to assume that formal organizations are rational actors who strive to optimize their self-interests in their respective environments (Yuchtman and Seashore, 1967; White, 1974; Aldrich and Pfeffer, 1976; Thompson, 1967).[7] In the vast literature on interorganizational relations, numerous researchers have shown how concern over organizational survival and autonomy shapes organizational behavior (e.g., Levine, White, and Paul, 1963; Allen, 1974; Levine, 1972). Indeed, organizations' overriding concern with their own self-interest is time-bound and culture-bound because it is certainly possible in other cultural contexts for collectivist values or norms to govern organizational interaction (see Taraki and Westby, 1976). It might even be suggested that the current emphasis on organizational self-interest is a sort of "ideology" itself that acts as a self-fulfilling prophecy for organizations today (see Warren, Rose, and Bergunder, 1974; Warren, 1971). Regardless, a norm of rational self-interest seems to prevail among organizations, and thus we feel comfortable working under this assumption.[8]

We also assume that organizations are open systems, and that, consequently, they must continuously engage in boundary interchanges with other organizations in their environment (see Parsons, 1956; Thompson, 1967; Katz and Kahn, 1966). No organization is totally self-sufficient, rather each must enter into interorganizational relationships with other organizations to secure those resources that it needs and to dispose of its outputs. Although organizations strive for functional autonomy, it is a state that is never fully realized (Gouldner, 1970; Guetzkow, 1966; Litwak and Hylton, 1962).

Working under these two general assumptions, formal organizations can be analyzed as purposive actors who attempt to dominate and control their environment in order to decrease uncertainty and increase their own influence over other actors. At the same time, they can also be analyzed as functionally dependent actors who must establish interorganizational linkages with others to secure those resources necessary for their own survival. While the desire to dominate others presses organizations to make other organizations dependent on them, the functional needs of these same organizations, in turn, make them dependent upon others.

We also argue that aggregations of different interorganizational dependency relations constitute key social structures in the community. These structures are not only relevant to the satisfaction of different functional needs of individual actors but also bind organizational actors into a common system of interdependencies (see Spergel, 1976).

Within each of these complex structures we can empirically identify the actors who occupy certain structural positions using standard sociometric methods. In Chapter 3 we describe the positioning of a wide range of organizations in interorganizational networks of money, information, and moral support, paying special attention to the actors who occupy central positions in the networks. In trying to figure out why some actors are more central than others, we will examine organizations' resources, structural dependency on the local community, and activities/functions. We will also analyze the proximities of organizations in these networks. For this analysis, organizational values, goals, and the local political environment will be examined as they affect interaction patterns within each interorganizational system.

Communities, like all social organizations, face the dilemma of exercising collective power. Applying our theoretical perspective to this problem, we will examine the behavior of formal organizations in five community issues. Because each of the interorganizational networks constitutes a social structure relevant to a different functional need of organizations, when a collective or community issue develops demanding a collective response, we expect that actors' positions in these network structures will be important in explaining their level of participation and their influence in community decision-making.

Chapter 4 will examine the effects of actors' centrality in each of these networks on their participation in the five issues. We will argue that being central in these structures puts an actor in a pivotal position with respect to different functional areas of community life. Thus, as different issues develop relevant to different functional needs, centrality in the respective interorganizational networks should be most important in predicting organizational activation.

In Chapter 5 we will examine the relative influence of organizations in community affairs. Hopefully, we will be able to explain why, across a number of decisions, some actors tend to be more successful than others. We expect to find that an actor's inflow and outflow transactions with other organizations are most important in converting or mobilizing other actors' resources into effective influence for his own cause.

Although we are studying only one community, we hope that our efforts will demonstrate the usefulness of our analytic strategies, and this, in turn, will offset our inability to generalize to larger, more complex systems. We also hope that this study will motivate others to apply our techniques to much different communities and even to different types of social organizations. Ultimately, our task is to formulate a set of theoretical and research strategies that can be used to study a wide range of social organizations.

NOTES

1. We recognize that certain relationships are mandated by law, prescribed by tradition, or are established on the basis of sentiment (e.g., love, loyalty, charisma, etc.). Our model is really applicable only when these other forms of social relationships are of minimal importance and actors are somewhat free to establish relationships on strictly instrumental, self-serving grounds (see Turk, 1973a).

2. This is not to espouse a "great man" theory of social change. Technological, demographic, and cultural conditions must be such that actors can exploit their environment for their own purposes. Actors can only choose among the alternatives available to them; however, whatever means are utilized, the purpose for their use must be traced to the interests of actors.

3. For a review of theories of social change, see Applebaum (1970), Moore (1963), Etzioni-Halevy and Etzioni (1973), and Martindale (1962).

4. There is some interest now in identifying different "conduits" in a social group. A conduit is a relational channel within a group that carries a special type of information, e.g., gossip, warnings of danger, market information, etc. (see Degh and Vazsonyi, 1975). As of yet, however, very little empirical research has been done on these.

5. Obviously there are actors who do quite well without the "blessings" of those around them, e.g., organized crime and extremist political movements. Our reply to this is to repeat that legitimacy is a variable and that some organizations have more of it than others.

6. The reader should remember that in the literature that two types of "power" are discussed. The power of an actor is the probability that it can get its way in interaction with others (e.g., Weber, 1947). In contrast, the power of collectivity is its capacity to engage in some sort of collective action (e.g., Parsons, 1963).

7. Whether the "rationality" which governs organizational behavior is programmed to enchance "organizational survival" or the interests of elites within the organization is an important issue that needs to be raised (see Laumann, Galaskiewicz, and Marsden, 1978; Galaskiewicz and Shatin, 1978; and Benson, 1977). In this study we will assume that the interests of the organization rather than the organization's leadership govern organizational policy. Recent work on organizational leadership (e.g., Zald and Berger, 1978), however, makes us more aware of the possible impacts of organizational elites on developments within the organization.

8. Again we must recognize that relationships among actors are, at times, bound by external constraints, such as laws (see Aldrich, 1976; Hall et al., 1977). Certainly, in these rare instances power dependency theory and functional dependency theory are inapplicable. We would add, however, that more often than not relationships become legal only after they have been routinized through more informal exchange processes.

Chapter 2

METHODOLOGY OF STUDYING LARGE SOCIAL STRUCTURES

The agenda set in Chapter 1 proposes a number of interesting methodological problems. Recently, there have been a number of studies of community interorganizational systems, and each has utilized a somewhat different approach. In any scientific endeavor there is a limit to the types of research methods that are appropriate for a given problem. Fortunately/unfortunately, in sociological inquiry there is often a great deal of leeway allowed. In this chapter, after a brief description of the research site, we will review these methods and judge how appropriate they are for our agenda. We will then outline the methods to be used in this study. We feel that our strategies are appropriate for the research questions we address; however, throughout the chapter we will point out some of their shortcomings. Rather than discredit our research, we hope that our comments will motivate researchers to solve some of the methodological problems we encounter and to arrive at more satisfactory ways of studying community social structures.

The chapter will be divided into three parts. First, we will describe the research site. We will review its history and compare it to other communities in its region. Certainly, in a case study we make no pretense that our findings can be generalized; ours is not to be taken as a "typical midwestern community" (cf., Lynd and Lynd, 1929). On the contrary, we view this community only as a social laboratory wherein we can observe social structure and social processes in detail.

Second, we will discuss how we operationalized the interorganizational networks of money, information, and support in the community. This section will review several different methodological strategies used by researchers in the past, and a short critique will be given for each. From our comments it will be apparent that new strategies are needed. Next, we will discuss how organizations were chosen for our study. Finally, we will review how the actual networks were described. In our study we utilized sociometric-type questions, graph theory, and multidimensional scaling to represent local interorganizational networks. These strategies were used for specific reasons that relate to our conceptualization of social structure developed in Chapter 1.

Finally, we will discuss the reliability and validity of the questions used to describe interorganizational resource flows among actors. Usually these tests are not included in a research monograph, yet our methodology is new, and it is imperative to give some evidence that respondents understood the questions asked of them. This is especially important in this study, since all our analyses are based on these relational data.

Research Site

In developing new theoretical and methodological strategies for studying social organizations it is often advantageous to choose small, simple systems for analysis (Laumann and Pappi, 1976; Clark, 1975). Such systems allow the researcher to examine carefully the patterns of relationships among actors documenting in detail their social behavior. Case studies also make it simpler for researchers to do longitudinal analyses. Furthermore, by choosing relatively "closed systems," we can better control for any effects from outside the social organization.[1]

The town we chose as our case community is called Towertown (a pseudonym).[2] We began our fieldwork in the fall of 1973 and finished collecting data in the fall of 1974.[3] A multitude of data sources were used ranging from structured questionnaires with organizational elites to government documents to newspaper files to informal chats with townspeople. None of the members of the research team lived in the community, rather we commuted every day from our home about 60 miles away. Since the author was directly involved in the data collection throughout, he was known quite well to local townspeople. However, none of the research staff ever became personally involved with any of the issues or organizations studied, nor were any of us identified with any one faction in the community.

Towertown is a medium-size community with a full-time population of 32,885 (1970). Although there is a metropolitan area of seven million people about 65 miles away, the town itself is relatively isolated, and its institutions, for the most part, have developed free from outside influences. Residents still tend to work, reside, and purchase most of their consumer goods locally. Until 1974 there was not even an expressway from the nearby metropolis to Towertown.

The history of Towertown is closely tied to agriculture. The place was first settled in 1837 as the site for a sawmill and grew as a trading center for the agricultural community. It was incorporated as a village in 1856 and became a city in 1877. Since this part of the "cornbelt" has been blessed with good soil and flat land, farmers have always been fairly well off and influential in the surrounding county. Even industry in the area developed around agricultural needs. There were some small factories from the start; however, barb wire production beginning in 1874 was the first major industry. Barb wire, of course, became an important product not only because of expanding agricultural production but also because of World War I. Today there is no barb wire production in Towertown, and the old "barb wire" family fortunes have very little influence in community affairs. There are, however, still a number of streets named after the old families reminding the local residents of their heritage.

By 1900 the town had grown to over 5,900 spurred on by the barb wire industry, and by this time there was an incipient working class drawn from the farm community and the eastern United States. Because of the distance from the central city, rail intersections, and large bodies of water, Towertown did not experience an in-migration of southern or eastern Europeans; and very few Blacks came up from the South to work in local industries. As a result, ethnicity plays almost no role in the affairs of the community. Religious differences also seem to be unimportant. Even after World War II there was no significant minority migration to Towertown even though absentee owned industries were moving into the area.

In 1895 the state awarded a charter for a state teacher's college to Towertown when the state legislature was given 67 acres of free land for the normal school by a local entrepreneur. In 1900 enrollment at the college was 218 with almost all students enrolled in education programs. In fact, the school could not award a Bachelor of Arts degree until 1955. It was in the 1950s and 1960s that the college experienced significant growth with the enrollment going from 2,569 in 1954 to 29,719 in 1968. At this point, the college became a multipurpose university with a well-rounded curriculum including 160 different majors. From 1968 to 1973 enrollment remained about the same.

The significance of the university's growth was that it introduced a new population of students and faculty to the community. The faculty was recruited nationally and the students came from the nearby metropolitan area bringing with them their "urban ways." In the early 1970s more and more students were being recruited from minority neighborhoods in the nearby central city.

This population has had an especially important political impact on the community. For example, at the time of our study there were seven city council positions, and university people held four. Two positions were held by students from the university, and two were held by university administrators. The other councilmen included an attorney, a store clerk, and a salesman. Although the mayor at the time of our study was a former small businessman, in 1977 (after we had completed our fieldwork) the wife of an associate dean at the university became mayor. In national political elections we can also see the growing influence of the university population. In the 1956 presidential election, nationally 57.37 percent of the electorate voted for Eisenhower and 41.96 percent voted for Stevenson; in the county in which Towertown is located, 75.65 percent voted Republican and 24.21 percent voted Democrat (Scammon, 1958). In the 1972 election the tables turned radically with 37.53 percent voting for McGovern and 60.69 percent for Nixon nationally; while 39.43 percent voted for McGovern and 60.25 percent voted for Nixon locally (Scammon, 1973). There is no doubt that the town experienced the influx of a population whose political beliefs were much more liberal and who had quite different origins than those of the local residents.[4]

Because of increasing farm production, the development of indigenous (and now internationally famous) farm-related industries, and the growth of the university, residents have prospered and the community has remained an attractive place to live. Looking at Table 2.1 we see that the community is clearly middle class in character. The median family income is greater than in other rural communities, and there is a high concentration of workers in professional and managerial occupations. We might add that nearly one-third of the working population is employed in public education. This sector has grown the most with the university employing over 3000 workers at the time of the study. Although earlier we claimed that there was a working class, we should note that the percentage of individuals employed in manufacturing is not quite as high as in other rural communities. With the opening of a superhighway linking Towertown to the metro area 65 miles away Towertown may become more and more involved in industrial manufacturing. Finally, we might note that the community is becoming more and more ethnically and racially heterogeneous over time.

Table 2.1: Selected Population Characteristics for Towertown (1960, 1970) and Nonmetropolitan Urbanized Places of 10,000 or more (1970) in Illinois

	Towertown		Nonmetropolitan Urbanized Places of 10,000 or more	
	1960[1]	1970[2]	1960[1]	1970[2]
Total population	18,486	32,949	732,009	694,581
Black	.29%	1.81%	3.87%	5.17%
Foreign born	5.02	3.49	11.04	1.95
Spanish speaking	—*	1.35	—*	1.32
Median family income	$6,602	$10,867	$6,124	$9,851
Median school years completed				
Males 25 years +	11.7	12.9	—**	12.2
Female 25 years +	12.1	12.6	—**	12.1
Total employed over 16 years	7,497	13,790	274,043	268,710
Professional, technical and kindred workers	14.27%	23.23%	12.33%	15.65%
Managers and administrators	7.20	5.90	8.26	7.62
Sales	7.24	7.24	8.14	7.33
Clerical	16.79	21.99	15.06	17.17
Craftsmen	12.36	7.97	14.28	13.10
Operatives	17.86	8.73	19.94	15.01
Transportation	—*	1.99	—*	3.34
Laborers	3.69	3.60	4.41	4.37
Farmers	.37	.25	.31	.21
Farm labor	1.01	.31	.46	.35
Services	12.95	17.85	10.72	14.65
Private household services	1.68	.93	1.98	1.21
Occupation not reported	4.55	.00	4.09	.00
Total employed	7,497	13,790	274,043	268,710
Agriculture	3.13%	.91%	1.09%	.87%
Manufacturing	29.58	16.79	31.77	28.95
Education-Government	20.55	31.81	—*	9.31
Education-Private	.63	3.22	—*	2.67
Public administration	2.52	1.86	3.30	3.46
Other	43.57	45.38	63.83	54.71

*Data are not available in the reports for 1960 for nonmetropolitan urban places of over 10,000 residents.

**The census only listed the median years of education for all adults (10.7) for nonmetropolitan urban places of over 10,000 residents.

1. Bureau of the Census, Characteristics of the Population, Vol. 1, U.S. Department of Commerce, 1960.

2. Bureau of the Census, Characteristics of the Population, Vol. 1, U.S. Department of Commerce, 1970.

Interorganizational Networks: Strategies of Measurement

Researchers have developed a number of strategies to measure interorganizational networks in the past fifteen years. In several literature reviews these are discussed both implicitly and explicitly at great length (see Negandhi, 1975; Marrett, 1971; Laumann, Galaskiewicz, and Marsden, 1978). In this section we will briefly review four general methods in use today and discuss some of their shortcomings. After our review, we will then outline how we operationalized interorganizational networks in our case community.

METHODS FOR INTERORGANIZATIONAL STRUCTURAL ANALYSIS

Most commonly, researchers have examined the egocentric networks of organizations. Following Evan (1966) this strategy examines those actors who make up a focal organization's immediate relational set. As Evan points out, the organizational set is analogous to Merton's (1957a) role set. This research design follows in the wake of contingency theory and research which examined how intraorganizational structures reacted to different environmental conditions (e.g., Lawrence and Lorsch, 1969; Thompson and McEwen, 1958). To study how pair-wise relationships were formed between organizations in response to environmental contingencies was a logical extension. A number of studies have used the pair-wise relationship as the unit of analysis (e.g., Aldrich, 1976; Hall et al., 1977; Allen, 1974; Galaskiewicz and Shatin, 1978), and this strategy seems to work quite well if the researcher is interested only in the effects of organizational characteristics and the immediate task environment on organizations' transactions. A further impetus for this type of analysis was given by those who wanted to apply exchange theory to the study of interorganizational relations (e.g., Levine and White, 1961; Adamek and Levin, 1975). Obviously there are drawbacks to studying only pair-wise relations between actors. As Warren (1967) and, more recently, Van de Ven et al. (1975) point out, one loses any sense of the social context and particularly the total network that organizations are enmeshed in.

Herman Turk (1970, 1973a, 1973b, 1977) has also looked at egocentric networks, but has broadened the analysis considerably. Looking at focal actors in a number of different cities, he describes how the "demands" put upon organizational networks by interests in the community result in certain "products" which come out of interorganizational joint action. His work has been particularly impressive, since his analyses have included 130 American cities. Recently, Galaskiewicz (1978) has undertaken a similar analysis with the NORC Permanent Community File of 51 cities. His focus is on organizational interest group contact with city officials and how this affected groups' "success" or "failure" in local community decision-making. This influence process was studied in several different community contexts. Unfortunately, there has been little other research in this mode. Perhaps the crudeness of available macrolevel interorganizational indicators has discouraged researchers (see Laumann, Galaskiewicz, Marsden, 1978). Obviously, comparative analyses of interorganizational network systems is at the top of any research agenda, and we certainly expect that more refined measures of interorganizational structure will be devised in the near future.

A third strategy is to look at complete subnetworks in a community. These subnetworks are similar to what Warren (1967) refers to as an interorganizational field. The current popularity of this research design lies in the researcher's ability to treat organizations as a system (Van de Ven, et al., 1975). Spergel (1976), Warren, Rose, and Bergunder (1974), Knoke and Rogers (1978), Rogers (1974), Bick and Muller (1978), and Galaskiewicz and Shatin (1978) all seek to describe various sorts of interorganizational "subsystems." Most of these research efforts have included a comparative analysis of several different communities. There are, of course, limitations to this approach as well; corporations do not only interact with other corporations and social welfare organizations do not only relate to other welfare agencies (Hall and Clark, 1975). On the contrary, organizations have direct and indirect linkages to a wide variety of organizations in their environment and these ought to be described also.

Finally, we find some attempts to describe quasi-complete interorganizational systems. All of these efforts have been made in conjunction with studies of community decision-making. Looking at formal organizations as powerful institutions and interest groups, Perrucci and Pilisuk (1970) and Laumann and Pappi (1976) have examined how overlapping memberships tend to draw certain interest groups into coalitions around certain issues. Much of this research borrows from Coleman's (1957) now classic work on community conflict. Perrucci and Pilisuk (1970) focus on the behavior of interorganizational elites, while Laumann and Pappi look at the relative social distance between organizations which take different positions on community issues. Freeman (1968) also examined a wide range of organizations in a community decision making context identifying coalitions on the basis of organizations' participation patterns in issues.

IDENTIFYING THE POPULATION

For our data on interorganizational linkages we went directly to representatives of a wide variety of organizations in the community. A representative list of formal organizations in Towertown was drawn up which included industries, service organizations, banks, savings and loans, unions, law firms, health agencies, high schools, colleges, universities, welfare agencies, churches, mass media, professional associations, business associations, county offices, municipal offices, and political parties.[5] We compiled this list from directories, telephone books, and interviews with local informants. Once an organization was selected, we identified the highest ranking executive officer and asked him/her to act as a spokesperson for the organization.[6] For ten organizations we interviewed two or more agents. We anticipated that this would give us an opportunity to check the reliability of our interorganizational questions. A comparison of responses to these questions is presented later in the chapter.

One hundred and nine organizations in the community met our selection criteria (see Table 2.2). At the completion of the interview period we had interviewed 73 out of the 109 organizations which were on the original list. The thirty-six organizations which were not interviewed included: ten unions (we interviewed four unions which we felt were representative of labor), twenty-two churches (we interviewed seven churches which we felt were representative of the town's religious denominations), a law firm (refusal), a cable television company, a medical association (disbanded), and a welfare association (disbanded).

Several authors have pointed out difficulties which often go along with the type of research design that we propose. First, it is not that easy to know where some organizations begin and end. As Laumann et al. (1978) point out, if the researcher is working with an ideal-typical Weberian bureaucracy, there is little difficulty identifying organizational boundaries, but if an open systems model of organizations is espoused, boundaries are a problem (Katz and Kahn, 1966). This problem becomes especially difficult in handling legally mandated organizational interaction (e.g., Aldrich, 1976; Hall et al., 1977). Governmental units also are problematic, since it is not always clear that units (e.g., police departments, fire departments, etc.) constitute separate organizations (see Klonglan et al., 1976). In our study, however, we treat different city departments as separate organizational entities (see Bick and Muller, 1978).

Laumann et al. (1978) also point out that problems of definition arise because a corporate actor is composed of persons who are affiliated with multiple roles and statuses.

[R]elationships which occur between persons in their capacities as agents of particular corporate actors must be distinguished from those which have an interpersonal or other basis. Such difficulties are probably minimized where interorganizational relations are formalized in devices such as contracts which specify that certain types of transactions are to be performed by parties to the agreement. In less obvious cases, behavior of boundary personnel must be scrutinized in order to determine the basis of their interaction with agents of other organizations (Laumann, Galaskiewicz, and Marsden, 1978).

For most absentee-owned and -controlled corporations and bureaucracies there is little danger that executives would be acting out roles other than their organizational roles. For local voluntary associations and city government offices there is greater danger that what may seem like interorganizational linkages are really interpersonal transactions.

Table 2.2: Original Organizational List (Pseudonyms)

Farm Bureau
Farm Equip Co.
Clothing Manufacturing
Co.
Farm Supply Co.
Mechanical Co.
Electric Equipment Co.
Metal Products Co.
Music Equipment Co.
Chamber of Commerce
Banker's Association
1st Towertown Bank
Towertown Savings
and Loan
Bank of Towertown
2nd Towertown Bank
Brinkman Law Firm
Cater Law Firm
Knapp Law Firm
Lenhart Law Firm
Bar Association
Board of Realtors
The Small Business
Association
Municipal Employees
Union I
Municipal Employees
Union II
Teachers' Union
Construction Council
Machinists' Union
Electrical Workers'
Union
Carriers' Union
Electricians' Union
Musical Instruments
Workers' Union
Plastic Workers' Union
Steel Workers' Union
Retail Workers' Union
Central Labor Union
Association of
Machinists
YMCA
City Council
City Managers' Office
County Board

Fire Department
Human Relations
Commission
Mayor's Office
Police Department
Sanitary District
Streets and Sanitation
Department
Park District
Zoning Board
Democratic Party
Organization
Republican Party
Organization
League of Women
Voters
Towertown News
WTWR Radio
Warner Cable Co.
Hospital Board
Public Hospital
Medical Society
Board of Mental Health
Mental Health
Association
County Board of Health
Health Services Center
Highway Authority
1st Kiwanis Club
2nd Kiwanis Club
Rotary Club
Lions Club
United Fund/
Community Chest
School Board
High School
Parent-Teacher
Association
Local Community
College
Employment Services
Towertown Mental
Health Center
State University
1st Association of
Churches
2nd Association of
Churches

University Catholic
Church
St. Hilary Catholic
Church
Advent Christian Church
Assembly of God
Bethel Baptist Church
Jerusalem Lutheran
Church
Church of Christ
Church of God
Church of the Savior
Evangical Testament
Church
Church of the Light
Towertown Christian
Church
Brotherhood Baptist
Church
1st Baptist Church
1st Church of God
1st Church of the Light
1st Congregational
Church
1st Lutheran Church
1st Methodist Church
The Gospel Church
Rosalie Lutheran Church
Advent Lutheran Church
Jehovah's Witnesses
Later Day Saints
St. Peter's Episcopal
Church
Church Road Baptist
Church
Unity Lutheran Church
Fellowship of
Towertown
University Methodist
Church
Towertown Welfare
Services
Department of Public
Aid
Family Services
Youth Services Bureau
Housing Authority

Setting the geographic community as the arbitrary boundary for interorganizational transactions is also problematic. Obviously, there are numerous ties with organizations outside the community, and these are often much more critical for organizations than local ties (see Levine and White, 1961; Warren, 1963; Spergel, 1976; Turk, 1977; Galaskiewicz and Shatin, 1978). As Hall and Clark (1975) argue, setting arbitrary boundaries on networks can have far-reaching effects on the "network" that the researcher finally ends up studying. In effect, the researcher is forced to choose either to set a priori limits based either on domain or geography (see Laumann et al., 1978) or use a variation of snowball sampling (e.g., Coleman et al., 1966). Neither method is completely satisfactory; and, as of yet, the problem of establishing network boundaries remains unsolved.

THE DESCRIPTION OF THE BASIC NETWORKS

Once the organizations and respondents in the community were identified, we had to describe the interorganizational transactions of money, information, and support. Of the several strategies which could have been employed, the one used seemed to us to be the most straightforward.[7] In the course of the interview, we handed the agent a list of the one hundred and nine organizations in Towertown and asked a series of questions to determine his/her organization's relations to all the other corporate actors on the list. The respondent was free to name as many organizations as s/he thought appropriate (see Appendix B, Q19 to Q24).

One problem with our questions is obvious from the start. We asked respondents to indicate simply which organizations their organization gave and received money, information, or support. We did not ask them to indicate "how much" money, information, or support they gave or received. During a pretest of these questions, we discovered that data on the "amount" of a transaction was very difficult to collect. First, this information was considered by respondents to be confidential. Many respondents pointed out that they were simply not at liberty to divulge, for example, how much money they gave or received annually from specific organizations. Even our promise of full confidentiality did not seem to allay their concern. Second, respondents found it difficult to "quantify" units of support and information. Attempts to operationalize units for these resources, e.g., frequency of phone calls, just seemed to confuse the respondent or misrepresent the situation as s/he saw it.

There are, of course, other dimensions of interorganizational exchange that our questions also ignored. Marrett (1971) argues that researchers ought to explore the degree to which relationships are formalized, the intensity of the interaction, the degree of reciprocity, and the degree of standardization. Aldrich (1976) and Hall et al. (1977) are two examples of how to achieve more exact measurement of interorganizational transactions. These dimensions are quite easy to measure when the dyad is the unit of analysis; however, there seems to be no serious problem with incorporating these factors into analyses of entire network systems. To date, there has been virtually no research on weighted, multiplex networks for a large population of organizations.

Graph theory (see Harary, Norman, and Cartwright, 1965) proved to be most helpful in constructing the networks of money, information, and support among the seventy-three organizations from the information provided by our sociometric questions. Its ready application to the study of empirical structures lent itself easily to our study of interorganizational systems (see Rogers, 1974; Cook, 1977; Laumann and Pappi, 1976). In order to help the reader better understand how we used graph theory and how it can be used in the future, let us review some key graph theoretic concepts that were employed in our study.

The study of structural relationships among social units was pioneered by Moreno (1953) and developed by a number of social psychologists. Their research was confined primarily to the study of small groups and friendship ties among individuals within these groups. The "sociogram" which they created is constructed by asking each member of the group to identify other members with whom he or she is friends. The set of relationships within the groups was then "mapped" in a two-dimensional space using points to represent the individual actors and directed lines or arrows to denote the directions of friendship choices. The sociogram for a hypothetical population of five actors specifying friendship ties is given in Figure 2.1. Actor A chose actor B and actor C, actor B chose actor C and actor E, actor C chose actor A, actor D chose actor C, and actor E chose actor B and actor D. The entire set of points and lines in Figure 2.1 is referred to as a sociogram but is equivalent to what graph theory calls a digraph.

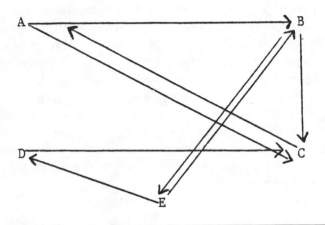

Figure 2.1: Example of Sociogram with Five Actors

	A	B	C	D	E
A	–	1	1	0	0
B	0	–	1	0	1
C	1	0	–	0	0
D	0	0	1	–	0
E	0	1	0	1	–

Figure 2.2: Adjacency Matrix of Sociogram in Figure 2.1

Using an adjacency matrix is another way to represent the above structure of social choices. An adjacency matrix A of a digraph D is a square matrix with one row and one column for each point of D, in which entry $a_{ij} = 1$ if the line $v_i v_j$ is in D and $a_{ij} = 0$ if $v_i v_j$ is not in D (Harary et al., 1965:15). The adjacency matrix for the digraph in Figure 1 is presented in Figure 2.[8] Once the set of relationships is translated into matrix form, it is now possible to use matrix algebra to manipulate the data allowing one to discover subtle structural properties of the network (e.g., White et al., 1976; Boorman and White, 1976).

Below are several definitions found in graph theory which may be useful to the reader (see Harary et al., 1965:404-410).

A *net* consists of a finite set of points together with a finite set of lines, where each line is an ordered pair of points.

A relation is *symmetric* if wherever there is an arc from v_i to v_j, then there is an arc from v_j to v_i; it is *asymmetric* if an arc from v_i to v_j precludes an arc from v_j to v_i.

A *path* from v_1 to v_n is a collection of distinct points, $v_1, v_2,..., v_n$, together with the lines $v_1 v_2, v_2 v_3,..., v_{n-1} v_n$.

A *length* of a path is the number of lines in it.

The *path distance* from v_i to v_j, $d(v_i, v_j)$, is the minimum length from v_i to v_j.

The *path distance matrix* of a digraph is the matrix whose entries are the path distances between all pairs of points.

For our purposes, each organization is represented by a "point" in a digraph and its relationship with another actor is represented by a "line." The "direction" of the arrow indicates whether an actor gives a particular resource to another or receives it from that actor.

We constructed three binary adjacency matrices representing interorganizational flows of money, information, and support respectively. In assigning values to the cells of our matrices, a flow in a given direction between a pair of organizations was said to be present if the agent of either organization in the pair mentioned it. For example, a flow of money was said to pass from actor A to actor B if either A mentioned that he had an outflow of money to

B or B mentioned that he had an inflow from A. Note that this decision rule retains the potential asymmetry of flows; it is merely a weaker criterion for measuring the presence of relationships than the alternative procedure of treating a flow as present only if it is reported by both organizations.

Our decision rule has certain advantages. First, it helps to compensate for respondent fatigue. The questions on corporate actor transactions came late in the interview, and the questions often became quite tedious as the respondent had to go through the group list a total of six times. Our interviewers reported that respondents often became restless after going through the list two or three times.

This rule also helps to correct for actors' different perceptions of transactions. Transactions between a large organization, such as a bank, and smaller organizations, such as a service organization, might be evaluated quite differently by the actors involved. The former might regard the transaction as trivial, while the latter might see it as very important for its survival. It is not inconceivable, then, that in an interview situation the larger actor might inadvertently overlook his transactions with the smaller organization. The "logical-or" criterion has the advantage of picking up these data which might otherwise be missed.

Finally, these rules help amend fraudulent answers. Several respondents commented on the sensitivity of the information and the importance of confidentiality. Even though the interviewers did assure respondents that their answers would be kept in the strictest confidence, we expect that some of our respondents were less than completely candid with us. Using a less stringent decision rule helps to correct for this "error," since the responses of other agents would make up for delinquent respondents.

SPATIAL REPRESENTATION OF THE NETWORKS

For our analyses we could simply look at the sociogram for each resource and the corresponding adjacency and path distance matrices. However, sociograms and matrices with seventy-three points are very difficult to interpret. An alternative strategy was to use any one of a number of current multidimensional scaling techniques (Guttman, 1968; Lingoes, 1973; Roskam and Lingoes, 1970). The one most appropriate for our analysis proves to be smallest space analysis–I (SSA-I).[9] SSA-I is a multidimensional scaling routine that maps points in an Euclidean space as a function of their respective proximities. One of its main advantages is that proximity measures need only be ordinally scaled. Points which are relatively "close" to one another on a given criterion will be located near one another in the solution, while points which are relatively "distant" from one another will be located far from one another in the solution. The "picture" one gets, then, is dependent on the proximity measure used. McFarland and Brown (1973) discuss the various types of measures available and their limitations. Because of the strictness of the monotonicity assumptions, it is critical that proximity measures remain faithful to a distance generating model.

For our subsequent analyses we use the symmetrized path distances as our proximity estimates. These distance measures meet all the above assumptions and, in our opinion, have the added advantage of being derived directly from the interaction of the organizations themselves (Laumann and Pappi, 1976). Actors which were reachable in a minimum number of steps were considered "closer" to one another, while those at greater path distances were considered "farther" apart.[10] Although there are other "distance" measures that we could have used, this seemed to us more appropriate given our research interests.[11]

Each of the three symmetrized path distance matrices were submitted to a precompiled FORTRAN program that performs smallest space analysis–I (Roskam and Lingoes, 1970; Lingoes, 1973). This program interprets the path distances as the true proximity measures and orders them monotonically. Through an interative procedure the program then attempts to discover an optimal solution that would represent the original ordered proximities in a minimum number of dimensions with the least distortion in the original rank order. Ideally, the program will produce a satisfactory solution in only two or three dimensions. In the SSA-I solutions for our three resource networks we had adequate fits in only two dimensions. The coefficient of alienation was .154 for the information SSA-I solution, .137 for the money solution, and .115 for the support solution.[12]

Obviously the biggest drawback to the use of SSA-I is that we are forced to symmetrize relationships between organizations. Although this may not have been too serious with respect to information, it is a problem with money and support transactions (see Galaskiewicz and Marsden, 1978). In light of this we should interpret our findings cautiously as interorganizational dependencies are not reflected in our smallest space solution. Distance between actors is based only on the presence or absence of a given type of resource transaction regardless of direction. Losing asymmetries is a serious price to pay in any relational analysis; however, we felt that the importance of retaining a distance measure that reflected the connectedness of organizations outweighed the obvious disadvantages of symmetrizing relationships.[13]

Problems of Reliability and Validity

Throughout our discussion we have pointed out a number of problems that researchers face in studying interorganizational systems. The methodology offered here certainly does not solve all of them; however, it does give the researcher another set of strategies. If our research design is to be used in the future, we should be fairly confident that the questions on interorganizational linkages are reliable, i.e., that they mean the same thing to different respondents who answer them; and that they are valid, i.e., that they truly give us a measure of what we want them to. In this final section we will offer tests of reliability and validity for our corporate actor questions. The reliability test examines the responses of two respondents in seven organizations and compares their responses to our questions. The validity test assesses the amount of agreement between the responses of organization v_i's agent which indicate the outflows of organization v_i and the responses of organization v_j's agent which describe the inflows to organization v_j.

We stated above that we had gathered data on interorganizational ties from more than one agent for ten of the organizations in Towertown; however, only seven of these ten will be discussed here.[14] Using the responses of the different agents we want to test the congruence of agents' responses to our corporate actor questions. If agents of the same organization give similar responses to our questions, then we could have more confidence that the questions were clear and the answers reasonably accurate descriptions of the organization's relations with others in the community.

The model that we used for this analysis is in Figure 2.3. "Agent 1" is the higher ranking officer or executive in the organization; "Agent 2" is a slightly lower ranking subordinate of "Agent 1." We did this analysis considering both inflows and outflows of all three media at once; thus the total number of possible ties that an organization could have to other actors in the community is 432.[15] The number of times that both agents reported that an asymmetric transaction had taken place between their organization and another was recorded in cell 1. The number of times that both reported no transaction with another organization was entered in cell 4. The number of times the principal agent (Agent 1) said that there was a transaction but the second agent did not mention it was recorded in cell 2. And, finally, the number of times a secondary agent (Agent 2) reported a relationship that was *not* mentioned by the first agent was entered in cell 3.

We see in Table 2.3 that there is actually considerable agreement in each of the seven organizations. For all of the cases, chi-square is significant at the .001-level, and the Q's are quite high. We might note from our inspection of the simple two-by-two tables that where there were appreciable discrepancies, typically it was the principal agent who had mentioned many more linkages than the subordinate. This supported our decision to record only

		Agent 2	
		Yes	No
Agent 1			
Yes		1	2
No		3	4

Figure 2.3: Model for Reliability Test

the responses of the higher ranking or principal agent in the organization. It seems that the higher ranking officer probably had the better overall knowledge of the organization's interorganizational ties.

Our test of validity is to look at all the organizations simultaneously and measure the extent to which reports of organizational "outflow" correspond to reports of organizational "inflow." If whenever organization v_i reports that it sends a particular resource to organization v_j, organization v_j reports that it receives that resource from organization v_i, then we have some reason to believe that both our questions on outflows and inflows are getting at the same thing. Obviously there are much better ways to test if our questions really describe the exchange of money, information, and support among organizations in our community, e.g., examining the accounts of different organizations and seeing just what sorts of money transactions have been recorded. Unfortunately, we did not have the resources to undertake such an analysis.

The analysis here is similar to the one above; only this time we do the analysis for one resource at a time. Taking the matrix which contains all the reported "outflows" of our seventy-three organizations for a given resource, we simply correlate it with the transpose of the matrix of inflows for that same resource.[16] Again a two-by-two table is used with "agreements" in the upper right hand and lower left hand cells, and discrepancies in the other two cells. The reader should remember that the reported pair-wise "relationship" is the unit of analysis, and for each table the total

Table 2.3: Tests of Reliability of Corporate Actor Questions for Seven Select Cases

	Chi-square	Sig.	Q
City department	92.81	<.001	.866
Church association	47.18	<.001	.791
Bank 1	44.07	<.001	.719
Bank 2	47.61	<.001	.821
Industrial firm	48.93	<.001	.916
Public decision-making body 1	58.94	<.001	.914
Public decision-making body 2	26.33	<.001	.784

Table 2.4:   Tests of Validity for Corporate Actor Questions for
             Three Resources

	Chi-square	Sig.	Q
Money	330.96	<.001	.802
Information	1124.87	<.001	.858
Support	512.51	<.001	.806

N is 5256.[17] Inflows and outflows with oneself (i.e., the diagonal elements) are not included in the analysis.

The chi-square statistics and Q's for the three resources are presented in Table 2.4. We are pleased to find that there is so much agreement between those who report "outflows" and those who report "inflows," since this gives us some confidence that our questions are getting at the right sort of thing. That is, when we ask for data on resource transactions in two different ways, we seem to be getting the same data.

Discussion

In this chapter we have described the research site in some detail, reviewed different research methodologies appropriate for the study of community interorganizational systems, and outlined the strategies which are used in this monograph to describe structural patterns among organizations in our case community. Throughout our discussion we have made an effort to be highly critical of ourselves and others in order to sensitize the reader to the problems involved in doing research of this sort.

Although we have probably raised more questions than we have answered we hope that the reader has not given up in despair. In the chapters that follow we will demonstrate how several very important substantive issues relating to interorganizational cooperation and conflict can be addressed using the structural data that we have in hand. Hopefully, we will also demonstrate how our operationalization of social structure helps us to bridge the gap between our theoretical conceptualization of structure as developed in Chapter 1 and the "real-life" world in which organizations carry on their day-to-day affairs.

Several of the methodological issues raised in this chapter will be discussed again in the concluding chapter. As we discover how well our research strategies are able to answer certain substantive questions, we will have a better idea of how to proceed with future research. In the meantime, let us proceed with the analysis of these networks and the structural positioning of actors in these networks. Hopefully, we have convinced the reader that the methods we used are credible and accurately represent the networks of relations among the organizations in Towertown. It is now for us to demonstrate how an understanding of these structures can help us to understand better the social organization of the community.

NOTES

1. Obviously, few U.S. communities are "closed systems" any more. Most of the community research before World War II (e.g., Lynd and Lynd, 1929) was preoccupied with documenting how even the very smallest cities were being drawn into a national division of labor. Research in the 1960s and 1970s has turned up little evidence that the trend is being reversed. Although outside influences can never be ignored, they can be minimized in studying more isolated social systems. In our research linkages to outside systems were only given passing attention, and this may be a serious problem. We believe, however, that the benefits of doing an intense analysis of structural patterns just within the community will compensate for our inattention to the role that the community plays in the national division of labor (cf., Turk, 1973a; Lincoln, 1977).

2. This community was not chosen at random. On the contrary, it had to meet several specific selection criteria. This study of interorganizational structure was done in conjunction with a comparative study of community elites conducted by Edward Laumann (see Laumann, Marsden and Galaskiewicz, 1977; Marsden and Laumann, 1977). In order to replicate his research on Altneustadt, Laumann needed to have a community which had a population of about 35,000, was somewhat distant from a large metropolitan center, and had a large research/educational facility that had brought in a more liberal, professional population into the community in the past few years. Towertown met all of these criteria.

3. The author was primarily responsible for collecting data for Laumann's study of Towertown's elite and, of course, his own data on local organizations. Peter Marsden and James Lynch assisted the author throughout the data collection phase of the project, administering interviews and collecting ethnographic data. It goes without saying that the present monograph would never have been possible without the conscientious efforts of the research team in the field.

4. There has been a number of community studies which have been in communities where there is a clear cleavage between "locals" and "cosmopolitans" (e.g., Merton,

1957b; Schulze, 1961). The reader might want to keep these studies in mind as s/he reads the substantive chapters that follow.

5. This obviously is not a complete list of all organizations in the town. It does not include retailers, block clubs, cooperatives, and several clubs and organizations within the organizations we did study. We restricted our list because of time and resource limits.

6. There were some exceptions. For a bank, the university, and one public decision-making body we used the responses of more than one agent. For one bank in the community we recorded the responses of two agents for money inflows and outflows. In this case the principal agent was particularly irked by the question regarding money flows. Consequently, we decided that it was necessary to supplement his set of responses. For the university we recorded the responses of three agents for support inflows and outflows. This decision also was based on the reluctance of the principal agent as well as his subordinates to answer our questions. Finally, for the city council, which had no clear ranking officer, we decided to record a response to a given corporate actor question if two or more council members concurred on an answer. Six out of seven council members were interviewed.

7. Interorganizational linkages of solidarity and information are often described by tracing shared memberships among organizations (see Perrucci and Pilisuk, 1970; Allen, 1974; Levine, 1972; Laumann and Pappi, 1976). The difficulty with this approach is that the researcher must infer that support and information are flowing through common members, but can never be really sure. Furthermore, these two resources are quite different, and thus we preferred to analyze their separate networks.

8. The reader might wonder why the diagonals are blank. We rationalized that by placing either a "1" or a "0" in the diagonal cell would be misleading, since we would be equating an intraorganizational linkages (i.e., an actor is linked to himself) with an interorganizational linkage. Unless specified otherwise, diagonals will be left blank in all analyses that follow.

9. For applications using smallest space analysis, see Laumann and Guttman, (1966), Blau and Duncan (1967), Laumann and House (1970), Levine (1972), Laumann (1973), Laumann and Pappi (1976), and Mortimer (1974). From these studies it is apparent that the methodology has a wide variety of applications.

10. All 73 organizations were mutually reachable in the three symmetrized path distance matrices. The maximum path distances for the information, money, and moral support digraphs were three, three, and five respectively.

11. There is a number of alternative measures available. The two most common types are based on the shared chracteristics of the actors themselves and the similarity of actors' relational set. The latter has received considerable attention recently. For discussion and examples of this latter type of distance measure, see Breiger, Boorman, and Arabie (1975), Burt (1976), and Lorrain and White (1971).

12. Generally, a coefficient of alienation less than .15 is considered to indicate a good fit. See McFarland and Brown (1973) for a detailed discussion of just what this coefficient is measuring.

13. Other programs in the smallest space analysis series are able to analyze asymmetric data (e.g., SSA-II). These programs were considered and our data matrices were analyzed with them. The results, however, gave us no new information that could not be gotten from examining the indegrees and outdegrees for each organization. For example, for the SSA-II row solution, organizations which received a large number of choices but had very few outflows were clustered in the center surrounded by those who had about

an equal number of inflows and outflows. On the periphery we had organizations which had many outflows but few inflows.

14. The choice of organizations for this analysis was not made in any systematic way. These seven organizations were selected because their chief executive officer and one of his/her immediate subordinates were included in Laumann's elite population and the subordinate was readily available to be asked the corporate actor linkages questions. There were three other organizations where we interviewed two or more agents—the city council, the newspaper, and the university. These were not included in this analysis, because for the newspaper the subordinate had given us data on only one linkage (information) and for the council we had six respondents and an analysis of all six would be too cumbersome for our purposes here. For the university we also had more than two respondents.

15. There are 432 possible ties for each organization, since there were 3 media inflows and outflows and 72 other actors in the community for one actor to interact with.

16. The matrices of reported outflows for information, money, and moral support are based simply on the responses to Q20, Q21, and Q23 respectively. The matrices of reported inflows for these same resources are based on the responses to Q19, Q22, and Q24 respectively.

17. The total number of asymmetric relationships is equal to $n*(n-1)$, where n is the total number of actors in the system. In our community, then, N is equal to 5,256.

Chapter 3

INTERORGANIZATIONAL RESOURCE NETWORKS: A SOCIAL STRUCTURAL ANALYSIS

In Chapter 1 we argued that certain structural properties of community institutions can be recovered by tracing the flows of selected resources among local organizations. We went on to argue that the formation of these networks is influenced by the interests of organizations in controlling their environment and satisfying their own functional needs. We would expect that the positions that organizations occupy in these networks would subsequently have an effect on their participation in community affairs and the probability of their "getting what they want" in different community decision-making situations.

Before we examine organizations' participation and influence patterns in community decision-making, we will focus on the

The author would like to thank the editors of *Social Forces* for allowing me to republish in this chapter some of the findings presented in my article, "Community organizational linkages," *Social Forces* (June) 1979.

structure of the networks themselves. An important part of our study is simply to describe those organizations which occupy different structural positions within community interorganizational systems. In this chapter we will specifically describe those organizations which are more central and more peripheral in each of the networks studied. We will examine clustering patterns among organizations as well.

Centrality and Proximity in Urban
Interorganizational Networks

We argued that interorganizational relationships, for the most part, are established by organizational elites who seek to protect their own organizations' self-interests in restrictive moral and legal environments (White, 1974). To secure their input and output boundaries (see Thompson, 1967) and to insure their survival in a competitive environment, organizations enter into exchange relationships with other organizations (see Yuchtman and Seashore, 1967; Cook, 1977; Levine and White, 1961; and Benson, 1975). These exchange transactions come to be institutionalized in order to reduce uncertainty in the organizations' environment and to maintain a competitive advantage over other organizations.

CENTRALITY AND DOMINANCE IN RESOURCE NETWORKS

Within a field of organizations, certain corporate actors come to enjoy certain advantages over other actors simply by virtue of their relational position vis-a-vis other organizations. The literature on interorganizational fields has suggested that central positions in community interorganizational networks provide special competitive advantages for incumbents (Benson, 1975; Laumann and Pappi, 1976; Cook, 1977; Rogers, 1974). By definition, actors in the center of a network have better access to all other actors in the system, while peripherally positioned actors are dependent upon centrally located actors for the continued maintenance of the relational system. The fact that actors are positioned differently within the structure does not imply that it is in equilibrium nor that actors are satisfied with their own relative position in the structure. We expect that the level of satisfaction with the network as it is will vary across community settings.[1]

Assuming that being central in an interorganizational network is advantageous for organizations, we will offer and test several "descriptive hypotheses" that discuss which organizations will be more central in each of the community interorganizational networks that we will study.[2] These hypotheses are based on a competitive model of interorganizational relations as outlined above. In general, we expect that organizations' resources and interests in the local community as well as their activities will be key factors in determining which organizations will be central and peripheral in money, information, and support networks.

H1: The greater the amount of expendable funds organizations control in the local community, the more central they will be in community interorganizational networks of money, information, and support.

H2: The greater the number of individuals affiliated with organizations locally, the more central they will be in community interorganizational networks of money, information, and support.

Control over money and control over a large number of people are two important resources that provide organizations great leeway in establishing interorganizational relations. Because money is a highly generalized resource; those who have it potentially have control over a wide range of events (Clark, 1968). This not only means that wealthy actors are better able to take the initiative in establishing interorganizational relationships, but that others perceive them as very attractive partners and seek to establish linkages with them. This, in turn, enables organizational elites to be more selective in choosing partners and to choose only those that will improve their overall position in the network.

Control over "people" has a similar effect. Not only does it enable an organization to establish more linkages; but, in an era of direct action politics, control over people is a potentially important political resource in its own right (e.g., Alinsky, 1969). The number of employees or members an organization can influence makes large organizations important political allies and/or targets for cooptation. Being an attractive "target," however, again gives organizational elites greater freedom and provides them with more options in their interorganizational field.

H3: The more dependent organizations are on the local community for their cash inflow, the more central they will be in community interorganizational networks of money, information, and support.

H4: Organizations headquartered in the community are more likely to be central in community interorganizational networks of money, information, and support.

The fact that an organization has resources which enable it to establish itself in a dominant position does not necessarily mean that it will; an organization must also have an interest in dominating local institutions. In general, organizations have a greater interest in dominating environments upon which they are dependent for resources, inasmuch as uncertainty in these environments is more threatening to them (Warren, 1967; Levine and White, 1961; Schulze, 1961; Warren, 1963). Thus, to the extent that the local community is an important source of funds or legitimacy, organizations will be interested in being central in local network systems. To insure continued money inflows, organizations must be able to plan and invest wisely. Therefore, they must be able to predict and control developments in various functional sectors of community life. To insure their legitimacy, locally based organizations must keep in touch with various sectors of the community in order to protect themselves from other local actors who might openly challenge the "good faith" of their policies and decisions.

H5: Organizations involved primarily in the production and distribution of consumer goods are more likely to be central in community interorganizational networks of money.

H6: Organizations oriented toward problem solving or coordination of other organizations are more likely to be central in the information networks.

H7: Organizations providing human services for the community are more likely to be central in support networks.

The positions of organizations will also reflect what they do. Because money, information, and support have a special functional significance, organizations which specialize in the production and distribution of consumer goods, general community problem solving, and human services will be more central in the respective interorganizational resource networks. This makes sense, since an organization's position in a network determines how much control it has over the flow of a particular resource. For example, manufacturers, retailers, and financial institutions perform important economic functions. Thus they have a greater need to control the distribution of money in an interorganizational system and will be more central in the money network. Public decision-making bodies, law firms, the media, and voluntary associations are more concerned with resolving group conflict and general community problem solving. Thus they seek better access to information about community affairs and will be more central in information networks. Finally, health, education, welfare, and religious organizations are more involved in providing human services which the community as a whole feels are important. Thus these organizations seek to maintain their legitimacy in the local community and will be more central in support networks.[3]

PROXIMITY AND STRUCTURAL DIFFERENTIATION IN RESOURCE NETWORKS

Of equal importance is the relative social distance between organizations in each of these relational subsystems (Laumann and Pappi, 1976). In analyzing the proximity of organizations in a relational system, we want to discover the bases for segregation. What is there about certain organizations that draws them together or that drives them apart? We expect that it varies depending upon the relationship that the researcher is studying. For example, we expect that when exchanging money, organizations will pay attention to the auspices of their partner, when exchanging information, they will pay more attention to their partner's operational goals, and when giving or receiving moral support, organizations will be more conscious of the values of the other organization's leaders.

H8: Organizations under similar auspices will tend to be more proximate in interorganizational networks of money.

In the money network, organizations under public auspices will interact more with other public organizations, while organizations under private auspices will interact with other private organizations. The auspices of organizations will be important in money systems because money has considerably more institutionalized constraints on its circulation than information and support. Most importantly, there is a number of legal constraints on the circulation of public funds. Research has shown that these constraints often severely limit organizational interaction (Levy et al., 1974; Aldrich, 1976; Hall et al., 1977). In Towertown this tight control over public monies will be reflected in a clear differentiation between publicly and privately funded organizations in the money exchange system.

H9: Organizations engaged in similar activities in the community will tend to be more proximate in interorganizational networks of information.

Actors who engage in similar activities or perform similar functions in the community will exchange information more regularly. These organizations are drawn together because they share a common interest in regulating competition and working out problems of organizational domain (Reid, 1964, 1969; Evan, 1966). This pattern has been found in many different social settings, but perhaps most graphically in Laumann and Pappi's (1976) analysis of overlapping memberships among organizations in Altneustadt. Since the exchange of information facilitates negotiation among organizations and the settlement of domain problems, we expect that in information systems organizations are more likely to seek out those who are engaged in similar activities.

H10: Organizations whose elites share similar ideologies will tend to be more proximate in interorganizational networks of support.

Organizational elites will tend to support other organizations whose elites have values similar to their own. There is a long debate in the organizational literature over the influence of leadership "styles" on organizational behavior (see Selznick, 1957; Hage and Dewar, 1973; Lieberson and O'Connor, 1972; Guest, 1962; Benson, 1977). We expect that leadership has more of an effect on support transactions than on money and information exchanges. Since the legitimacy of organizations is established in the interorganizational field through expressions of moral support among organizational elites, the exchange of this medium is more likely to reflect the social, political, and economic values of the elites. We doubt that organizations are legitimated by being evaluated against a fixed set of collective values. Rather we suspect that the process is more interactive where an organization's elite decides to support one organization rather than another simply because an organization better reflects its own set of values. If we are correct, then the solidarity of organizations is based on shared ideologies, and in the support network we will find clusters of organizations whose leaders have very similar values.

Operationalization of Variables

In Chapter 2 we discussed how we recovered the interorganizational networks of money, information, and support. With several hypotheses related to the centrality and proximity of organizations, there is now a number of other variables that need to be operationalized. First, we must be able to identify what organizations are central and peripheral in the networks; and, second, we need to measure proximity or social distance between pairs of organizations. Along with these "positional" variables, several characteristics of the organizations must also be measured.

A centrality score for each organization in each network was computed directly from the SSA-I solutions for money (MONEY), information (INFOR), and moral support (SUPPORT). SSA-I locates the centroid of the space and computes the Euclidean distance from each actor/point in the two-dimensional solution to the centroid. (Roskam and Lingoes, 1970). This distance was used as our measure of an organization's "centrality." To check on the validity of this measure, we also computed the average path distance from each organization to all other organizations and correlated these new centrality measures with the centrality scores from the SSA-I solutions.[4] The Pearson correlations were .868, .784, and .857 for the information, money, and support networks respectively. Since it appears that SSA-I does not seriously distort the relative reachability among actors, we will use only the measures based on the SSA-I solutions for the analyses in this study.

The relative distance between organizations, or their proximity, in each of these networks was measured by computing the Euclidean interpoint distance between them in each of the respective SSA-1 solutions (PROXMON, PROXINF, PROXSUP) [see Laumann, Marsden, and Galaskiewicz, 1977]. Since the original proximity estimates are based on the path distances between organizations, the "distance" in the SSA-I solution reflects how readily two actors can "reach" one another. We might remind the reader that the coefficients of alienation for each of our networks were quite low, thus indicating the validity of this measure of social distance.

Data were also gathered on several characteristics of the organizations themselves. To ascertain which organizations had a greater interest in the local community, organizational informants were asked to indicate the percentage of their organization's income from the past year that came from the county in which Tower-town was located; this included sales, fees, grants, and gifts [INFL] (see Appendix C-Q8).[5] We also noted whether an organization's headquarters were located in the local community or elsewhere (HDQTLOC). To measure the amount of resources organizations controlled, agents were asked to tell us the total number of employees and members in their organization in Tower-

Table 3.1: Classification of Organizations According to Function

Economic (ECON)	Problem Solving (PROBLEM)	Human Service (SERVICE)
Manufacturing firms (7)	Business associations (5)	Municipal services (4)
Banks and savings and	Law firms (3)	Health services (3)
loans (4)	Professional associations (5)	Educational
	Labor organizations (4)	services (3)
	Public decision-making	Churches (7)
	bodies (11)	Welfare services (3)
	Political organizations (3)	Youth services (3)
	Mass media (2)	Highway services
	Service clubs (4)	
	United fund	

town [PERS] (see Appendix C-Q3 and Q3a)[6] and the total amount of expendable funds in Towertown over which their organization had control; this included funds for purchasing and salaries (FUNDS).[7] We also asked respondents about the percentage of their total cash inflow that came from governmental sources [PUBL] (see Appendix C-Q7).[8] If organizations received more than half their funds from governmental sources, they were considered public organizations. Since most of these variables were highly skewed, we recoded them to get more normal distributions.

Table 3.2: Recodes and Frequency Distribution of Selected Organizational Variables

INFL	Code	F	HDQTLOC	Code	F
0.0% – 84.9%	0	25	Headquarters outside		
85.0% – 100.0%	1	45	area	0	29
MD		3	Headqarters local	1	44
		73	MD		0
					73

FUNDS		Code	F	PERS	Code	F
$ 0 –	4,999	1	16	0 – 9	1	12
5,000 –	19,999	2	4	10 – 24	2	6
20,000 –	49,999	3	6	25 – 49	3	8
50,000 –	199,999	4	14	50 – 74	4	11
200,000 –	499,999	5	5	75 – 99	5	3
500,000 –	999,999	6	4	100 – 249	6	12
1,000,000 –	4,999,999	7	14	250 – 499	7	8
5,000,000 –	100,000,000	8	5	500 – 2000	8	12
MD			5	MD		1
			73			73

PUBL	Code	F	ACTIVITIES	Code	F
0.0% – 50.0%	0	51	Economic		
50.1% – 100.0%	1	22	organizations	1	11
MD		0	Problem-solving		
		73	organizations	2	38
			Human services		
			organizations	3	24
			MD		0
					73

We also classified organizations according to their activities or functions. We identified organizations as either engaged in manufacturing/finance (ECON), community problem solving/coordination (PROBLEM), or providing human services (SERVICE). Our classification of organizations is presented in Table 3.1. The recodes and frequency distributions for all these organizational variables are in Table 3.2.

Finally, we gathered data on the social and political values of the chief executive of each organization. In a set of twenty-three questions, respondents were asked if they agreed or disagreed with different viewpoints on selected social, political, and economic issues. Respondents were also asked to indicate from a list of seven "community goals" the three goals they considered to be most important for their community and the one they regarded as the least important. From these two sets of items, seven value scales for each respondent were constructed measuring attitudes on government intervention in the economy, civil liberties, religious traditionalism, family traditionalism, unions, social equality, and community goals. Appendix D describes the way we constructed these scales and gives the frequency distribution for these seven scales.

Money, Information, and Support Networks: An Overview

Figures 3.1, 3.2, and 3.3 present the two dimensional smallest space solutions for money, information, and moral support respectively. Before turning to our statistical analysis of centrality and proximity, let us look at these figures more closely. What is immediately apparent is that each network is structured quite differently.

The money network is clearly differentiated into public and private sectors. In the public sector, the positioning of actors is quite straightforward. In both the city and county/regional areas, decision-making bodies are more towards the center of the space (e.g., city council, sanitary district, county board, and school board), and governmental agencies are scattered around them. In the City Services sector the flow of money seems to follow a very

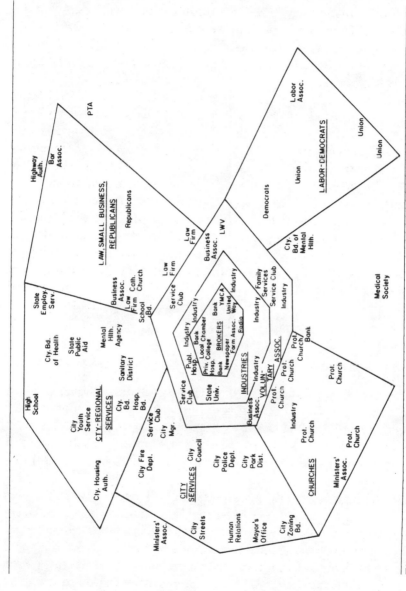

Figure 3.1: SSA-1 Solution for the Money Network

71

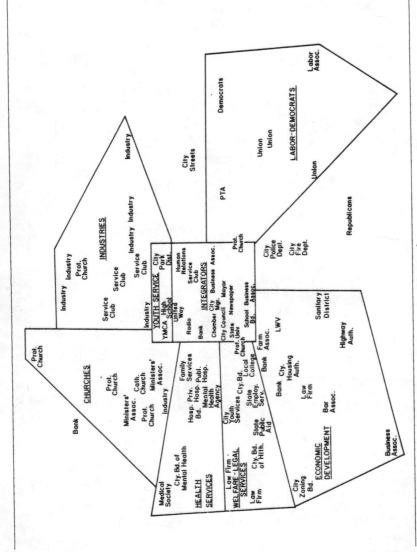

Figure 3.2: SSA-1 Solution for the Information Network

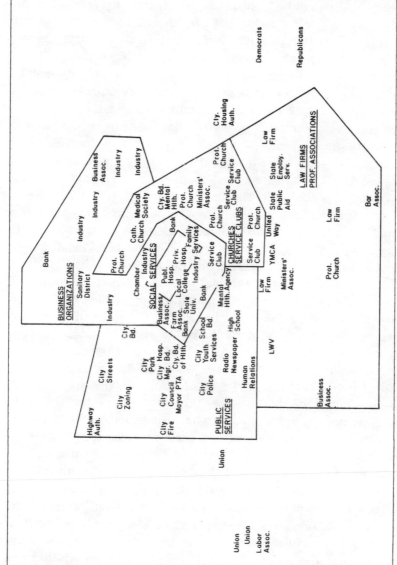

Figure 3.3: SSA-1 Solution for the Support Network

simple pattern: the council collects public tax dollars and redis-
tributes them to the different city departments and offices. On the
average, 91.3 percent of the funds which the city agencies in this
sector receive are from local sources, and they spend, on the
average, 98.5 percent of their revenue within the county. The only
"outside" money which comes to city agencies and offices is
through revenue sharing, which the city council and city manager
monitor. In the County-Regional Services sector the flow of
money appears to be more circumvented. Unlike the city council
which receives about 91.0 percent of its funds from local sources,
the county board receives only 80.0 percent of its funds from
local sources, and the school board gets only 73.0 percent of its
funds locally. The balance comes from state and federal programs.
The county agencies and the local high school similarly are not
solely dependent on local revenues. Excluding the housing authority and the hospital board, these organizations receive, on the
average, only 62.2 percent of their funds from local sources,
although they spend 97.2 percent of their funds locally.[9]

The organization of the private sector is more complex. To
begin with, there are three concentric zones in the center of this
sector: a zone of Brokers (e.g., banks, the Chamber of Commerce,
the United Way, and the mass media), a zone of Industries (both
local and absentee), and a zone of Voluntary Associations. Scattered throughout these zones are the YMCA, a private hospital,
the local public hospital, and a local family service agency. Interestingly enough, on the average, 92.3 percent of the funds that
these four health and welfare organizations receive are from private sources and 81.2 percent of their revenue comes from the
local community. It seems that these actors are located towards
the center of the money network in order to maintain their ties to
the important suppliers of private funds in the community. On the
periphery of the private sector, we find three traditional cluster-
ings of organizations. On the upper right there is a law firm/busi-
ness/Republican cluster, on the lower right a labor/Democrat
cluster, and at the lower left a church/ministers' association cluster.

The interesting positioning of organizations in this network
prompted us to see if there was some sort of division of labor in

this network. It seemed likely that certain organizations may perform specialized "functions" in the network. For example, within the three concentric zones in the private sector it seems reasonable that industries and service clubs might be important "generators" of funds for other organizations in the community (Form and Miller, 1960; Warren, 1963; Schulze, 1961; Mott, 1970); banks may be important "transmitters" of money; and social service agencies may be primarily "consumers" of revenue from other organizations (Warren, 1963).

To see if there was some division of labor, we went back to the original asymmetric adjacency matrix for money transactions and computed ratio coefficients for money inflows and outflows for different groupings of organizations; coefficients for the other media were computed as well. From these coefficients we could determine if different groupings were generators of funds (i.e., had more outflows than inflows), consumers of funds (i.e., had more inflows than outflows), or transmitters of funds (i.e., had about as many inflows as outflows).[10] The findings in Table 3.3 are what we might expect. Industries and service clubs are indeed important generators of funds (but so are churches and labor unions in the private sector and the city council/city manager in the public sector). On the other hand, health, education, and youth organizations (as well as the United Fund and the Chamber) are the biggest consumers of funds in the community. Finally, business associations, city administrative offices, and the PTA are obvious transmitters of funds.

The information network is organized according to a quite different set of principles. Here we find organizations clustered by activities rather than by auspices. To begin with, organizations engaged in general community problem solving are found in the center of the space (Integrators). The city manager's office, the mayor, and the city council are almost exactly in the middle of the picture. The mass media, the Chamber of Commerce, and the United Way are also in the center of the network. All of these organizations are very likely clearing houses, which more peripheral actors use to communicate with others in the community, as well as organizations which help to resolve community conflict.

Around the central core of communitywide problem solvers, there are specialized clusters of organizations. At the lower left of

Table 3.3: Functional Status of Corporate Actors in Three Networks

	Money			Information			Support		
	In	Out	r_i	In	Out	r_i	In	Out	r_i
Industries (7)	15	74	-.633[a]	80	90	-.058	43	55	-.123
Banks (4)	120	79	.206	93	89	.022	36	73	-.339[a]
Business assoc. (4)	21	22	-.023	66	68	-.014	26	58	-.381[a]
Labor (4)	4	13	-.529[a]	30	34	-.062	15	19	-.118
University (1)	13	7	.300	30	35	-.077	42	20	.354[b]
United Fund (1)	17	4	.619[b]	16	16	.000	15	6	.428[b]
Law (3)	28	48	-.263	44	50	-.063	17	25	-.190
Political parties (2)	8	5	.230	7	9	-.125	1	2	-.333[a]
Service clubs (5)	16	38	-.407[a]	61	69	-.061	42	67	-.229
Decision-making body (7)	38	47	-.106	155	145	.033	95	88	.034
Publ. information (2)	6	15	-.428[a]	64	62	.023	29	26	.052

Table 3.3: Functional Status of Corporate Actors in Three Networks (Cont.)

	Money			Information			Support		
	In	Out	r_i	In	Out	r_i	In	Out	r_i
Media (2)	34	46	-.150	124	110	.060	12	35	-.490[a]
Chamber (1)	15	6	.428[b]	37	36	.014	20	24	-.091
Administration (9)	26	25	.019	130	130	.000	84	43	.323
Prof. assoc. (4)	9	5	.286	51	50	.010	43	48	-.055
Church (7)	11	40	-.568[a]	105	72	.186	45	88	-.324
Health (3)	45	21	.364[b]	66	79	-.090	80	41	.322
Education (2)	20	7	.481[b]	29	41	-.172	75	70	.034
Youth (4)	69	13	.683[b]	98	100	-.010	98	70	.622[b]
PTA (1)	2	2	.000	10	11	-.048	12	4	.500[b]

a. Generator
b. Consumer

the space we find organizations primarily involved in the economic development of the community. The banks and the farmers' association are obviously concerned with economic development. However, we also find a number of public sector actors as well: for example, the sanitary district, the highway authority, the housing authority, and the zoning board. To the left of center we find clusters of organizations concerned with different types of human services. There is a cluster of law firms and organizations concerned with providing a variety of social services; there is a cluster of hospitals, health agencies, and health boards; and we find a cluster of churches. At the top of the space there is a cluster of industries and service clubs. And, finally, at the right of the space there is a cluster of labor unions and democrats.

This pattern of "sectoral differentiation" seems to be supported by several specialized private regulatory agencies in each of the sectors. Just as affairs of the whole community may be integrated through organizations in the center of the network, the affairs of specialized sectors may be integrated through sector-specific control agents. We see that the bankers' association and the bar association are located in the middle of the Economic Development sector; the medical society is in the Health Services sector; ministers' associations are in the Churches sector; service clubs are in the Industries sector; and the labor association is at the periphery of the Labor-Democrats sector. Of course, we have no proof that these organizations do indeed perform coordinating functions in each of these sectors. Their more peripheral position in the overall network may be as much a testimonial to their impotence as to their coordinating ability.

The support network does not appear to be organized around one set of principles like the other two networks. In the center of the space we find organizations which provide health and educational services (Social Service) (e.g., two local hospitals, a local family service agency, and the local college), while organizations representing special interests are on the periphery (e.g., business organizations, unions, and political parties). Similar to the money network, there seems to be a distinction between public and private organizations, and businesses and service clubs again flank organizations in the center of the private sector. Interestingly enough, this is the first time we see churches and service clubs relatively close to one another.

If we look a little closer at the network, we can divide public and private sectors in half and discover that in the upper half of the space we have a group of "material goods" organizations, while in the lower half we find "people-processing" organizations. Examples of the former include the industries, the sanitary district, the county board, city streets, city parks, city zoning, the highway authority, and city fire. The latter includes service clubs, churches, law firms, and both public and private health, education, and welfare organizations. It seems that the "raw materials" of organizations have some effect on which organizations elites will support.

Looking at Table 3.3 again, we see that the division of labor in this network is also similar to that found in the money network earlier. We find that the biggest consumers of support are youth agencies, the PTA, the United Fund, and the University. Health agencies and city administrative offices are not far behind. In contrast, the generators of support are the banks, the business associations, political parties, and the mass media. These are followed by the service clubs and the churches. That the same organizations tend to play similar roles in both the money and support networks suggests that certain institutionalized positions may well exist among organizations in this community (see Burt, 1976; 1977a; 1977b).

Centrality

We said earlier that centrality in these networks provides incumbents with certain advantages. Therefore, we hypothesized that organizations which had a greater interest in the community or which had control over greater amounts of resources would be in the centers of these networks. To see the independent effects of these variables on the centrality of organizations, we performed a simple regression analysis using the centrality scores for each of our three SSA-I solutions as the dependent variables.

Table 3.4: Zero-Order Pearson Correlations Among Organizational and Centrality Variables

	FUNDS	PERS	INFL	HDQTLOC	ECON	PROBLEM	SERVICE	MONEY	INFOR	SUPPORT	MEAN	SD	RANGE
Organizational resources													
FUNDS	1.000										4.19	2.41	1–8
PERS	.255	1.000									4.60	2.46	1–8
Organizational dependency													
INFL	-.614	-.137	1.000								.64	.48	0–1
HDQTLOC	-.200	-.376	-.203	1.000							.60	.49	0–1
Organizational technology													
ECON	.452	.149	-.377	-.049	1.000						.15	.36	0–1
PROBLEM	-.527	-.144	.431	.005	-.439	1.000					.52	.50	0–1
SERVICE	.220	.040	-.177	.032	-.295	-.729	1.000				.32	.47	0–1
Centrality in SSA-I solutions													
MONEY	.582	.230	-.161	.091	.343	-.193	-.056	1.000			51.83	30.80	6.4–119.3
INFOR	.343	.099	.096	.198	-.071	-.027	.083	.506	1.000		48.29	27.25	1.1–127.8
SUPPORT	.469	.121	-.093	.263	.073	-.247	.207	.552	.674	1.000	29.83	23.67	2.3–107.0

Table 3.4 presents the zero-order correlations for our measures of interest in the local community (INFL, HDQTLOC), organizational resources (FUNDS, PERS), and organizational activities (ECON, PROBLEM and SERVICE). We should note that INFL, HDQTLOC, ECON, PROBLEM, and SERVICE are all dummy variables. Table 3.4 also presents the zero-order correlations between our independent variables and our three centrality scores.[11] Looking at the two local interest variables first, HDQTLOC is positively correlated with each of our centrality measures, while INFL is negatively correlated with MONEY and SUPPORT. Looking at the resource variables, both FUNDS and PERS are positively correlated with each centrality measure. Furthermore, we see that ECON is positively correlated with MONEY and SERVICE with SUPPORT. Except for the zero-order correlations between INFL and centrality in the money and support networks and between PROBLEM and centrality in the information network, all our hypotheses are supported.

Table 3.5: Beta Coefficients Using SSA-I Centrality Scores as Dependent Variables

	Centrality in the Money Network MONEY	Centrality in the Information Network INFOR	Centrality in the Support Network SUPPORT
Organizational resources			
FUNDS	.684	.638	.574
PERS	.107	.098	.115
Organizational dependency			
INFL	.345	.496	.351
HDQTLOC	.072	.207	.258
Organizational technology			
ECON	.152	–	–
PROBLEM	–	.108	–
SERVICE	–	–	.129
Multiple R	.653	.561	.587
R Square	.426	.314	.345

Table 3.5 presents the multiple regression analyses with MONEY, INFOR, and SUPPORT as dependent variables. We see that our models explain 42.6 percent, 31.4 percent, and 34.5 percent of the variation in the money, information, and support centrality scores respectively.[12]

In contrast to our zero-order correlations, we see that INFL has a positive effect on each of the dependent variables, and that its effect is stronger than HDQTLOC in each case. From this we can conclude that organizations in the center of each of our networks tend to be heavily dependent on the local community for their financial support, and, to a lesser extent, they tend to be head-quartered locally. The standardized effects of both our resource variables, FUNDS and PERS, also support our hypotheses. It is clear that wealthier organizations and larger organizations tend to be more central in each of our networks than smaller, less wealthy organizations. Finally, we also see that economic organizations tend to be central in the money network, that problem-solving organizations tend to be central in the information network, and that human service organizations tend to be central in the support network. The effects of these latter variables are important; however, they are much weaker than the other effects just alluded to.

Proximity

From our visual inspection of the SSA-I solutions we have already learned that the social organization of the three network systems are quite different. Most of what we found was in line with our expectations. Now we would like to do a series of regression analyses to test more rigorously our hypotheses regarding the proximities of organizations in each network. More specifically, we will test the effects of organizational auspices, function, and value homophyly among organizational elites on organizations' proximities in the money, information, and support networks.

For this analysis we had to measure several variables for each *pair* of organizations in the network. Since we included only 60 of the 73 organizations, our N was 60(59)/2=1770.[13] A proximity measure for similarity of activities/function was derived by assign-

Table 3.6: Means, Ranges, Standard Deviations, and the Intercorrelations Matrix of Six Proximity Measures

	FUNC	AUSPICES	VALUE	PROXMON	PROXINF	PROXSUP	MEAN	RANGE	S.D.
Similarity of function (FUNC)	1.000						.63	0.0–1.0	.48
Similarity of auspices (AUSPICES)	.021	1.000					.41	0.0–1.0	.49
Value homophyly (VALUE)	-.007	.060	1.000				.97	.1–2.2	.387
Proximity in the money network (PROXMON)	-.050	.201	.221	1.000			.72	0.0–2.1	.39
Proximity in the information network (PROXINF)	.038	-.055	.071	.294	1.000		.67	0.0–1.9	.34
Proximity in the support network (PROXSUP)	-.027	-.054	.171	.309	.442	1.000	.39	0.0–2.0	.25

ing the value "0" to a pair of organizations if they engaged in the same activity and "1" if they did not (FUNC). For this variable we used the assignments presented in Table 3.1 to identify an organization's function. A proximity measure for auspices was derived by assigning the value "0" to a pair of organizations if they were both mostly funded by public funds or both mostly funded by private funds, and "1" if they were funded by different sources (AUSPICES). The percentage of organizational funds from public sources (PUBL) was used to identify where organizations received their money. Finally, value homophyly among leaders was measured by summing the absolute differences in the respondents' scores on the seven value scales discussed earlier in the chapter, submitting these as proximity estimates to a SSA-I, and computing the Euclidean interpoint distances between organizations in the value space (VALUE).[14] The means, ranges, and standard deviations for all these variables, along with their intercorrelations, are presented in Table 3.6 (see Appendix D).

Turning directly to the regression analysis in Table 3.7, we see that both similarity of auspices (AUSP) and similarity of values (VALUE) have a positive effect on proximity in the SSA-I solution for money. In other words, organizations which receive their funds from similar sources (whether they be private or public), as well as organizations whose leaders have similar values, tend to be at a lesser social distance in the money network. The effect of AUSP is not surprising since we hypothesized it and found it in our visual inspection of the SSA-I solution. On the other hand, the

Table 3.7:   Beta Coefficient Using SSA-I Interpoint Distances as
             Dependent Variables

	Proximity in the Money Network PROXMON	Proximity in the Information Network PROXINF	Proximity in the Support Network PROXSUP
AUSPICES	.190	-.060	-.064
FUNC	-.053	.040	-.025
VALUE	.210	.075	.174
Multiple R	.296	.101	.184
R square	.087	.010	.034

positive effect of VALUE is totally unexpected. For very instrumental transactions, such as money exchanges, leadership values should have no effect at all. Especially in a very "stable" community as Towertown, where leadership styles should be subsumed to the routine functional needs of the organization, a strong effect of values on money transactions is all the more curious.

At first glance, our findings for the information network are less encouraging: in the regression analysis similarity of function (FUNC) is only weakly related to proximity in the information SSA-I solution. The reader should remember, though, that we did find highly specialized clusters in our visual inspection of the SSA-I solution for this resource. Evidently, our measure of functional similarity (FUNC) is too crude to pick up the number of specialities found within our population of organizations. We find also that VALUE has a weak positive effect on proximity in this network; while AUSP has a weak negative effect. The implications of these findings are that the values of organizational leaders again affect the establishment of interorganizational ties, as we found in the money network but that the ties between organizations cut across organizational auspices rather than being constrained by them.

Finally, the analysis of the support space shows us that our measure of value homophyly (VALUE) has a positive effect on proximity in this network. That is, organizations tend to support other organizations whose leaders' values reflect the values of their own leadership. This is especially interesting in light of our earlier finding that organizations with similar technologies tend to cluster in the support space. Looking at the effects of the other two variables, we see that they have only very weak effects on PROXSUP. This, of course, is what we had expected.

Discussion

It was apparent in each of our analyses that these networks are highly structured. Through a visual inspection of the networks we were able to identify obvious structural differences across our networks. We were even able to identify a rudimentary division of labor that actors seemed to have worked out among themselves. In the money and support networks we were able to identify subgroups of organizations which acted as "generators," "consumers," and "transmitters" for other organizations in the community.

In our analyses of centrality, we likewise discovered a number of regularities in our networks. It was apparent that the resources and interests of organizations were very influential in structuring dominance patterns in community interorganizational networks. Wealthier organizations and organizations which were dependent on the local community for financial support were especially central in each of our networks. Larger organizations and organizations headquartered locally also tended to be more central.

We also found that organizational activities/functions had an independent effect on centrality. Constructing simple, common sense categories, we classified organizations as economic actors, problem-solving organizations, and human service organizations. We found that industries and financial institutions tended to be more central in the money network; community decision-making bodies, voluntary associations, the mass media, and law firms tended to be more central in the information network; and human service organizations tended to be more central in the support network. We suspect that the core technologies of these different organizations were important here; and this is what, in turn, explained centrality in the respective networks.

The proximity analysis introduced another set of factors that contribute to the social organization of these networks. We found that organizational elites employ different calculi when interacting via different media, thus giving rise to different clustering patterns within the networks. When engaged in money transactions, decision-makers will take into account the auspices of the other organizations in their field. On the other hand, when exchanging information, decision-makers will more likely seek out organizations on the basis of the activities they are engaged in. Finally, when establishing support linkages, organizational elites are more interested in the social values of other organizations' elites.

In light of our findings, I think that we can begin to appreciate just how complicated community relational systems are. We can also begin to understand how they come about. For the most part, the networks among organizations in a community are emergent phenomena. Although some aspects of interorganizational exchange are affected by legal mandates (e.g., the exchange of money), for the most part the social order seems to be the product of each actor pursuing his own narrowly defined self-interests and negotiating a set of working relationships with his neighbor (see Turk, 1973a).

If this is true, we can indeed marvel at the order we find. Hierarchies of dominance among organizations clearly emerged, while at the same time we found clusters that reflected the different specialized activities of organizations, the legal constraints in the environment, and the values of organizational decision-makers. We are at first tempted to extol the wonders of the "invisible hand" which brought about all this "order." Upon reflection, however, we would rather marvel at the ways in which the media of money, information, and support effectively structure interaction among organizations. As mechanisms to help actors in a social organization mediate their relationships with one another relevant to different functional needs, they seem to solicit interaction which brings about a certain order in the system. At this point, we do not know just how or why these symbolic media of exchange influence actors as they do. We can only guess that their generalized nature allows them to be readily manipulated allowing for the establishment of clearly differentiated hierarchies in social organizations, while at the same time their symbolic meanings draw together certain types of actors who need to satisfy certain functional needs. Regardless, our findings suggest that they have an important effect on how relational systems are organized.

For a structural analysis such as ours, simply describing the impact of the different media on interaction is sufficient, and this certainly contributes to our understanding of relational systems. From a social change perspective, however, this raises a number of interesting questions. What strikes us immediately is that the institutionalized media of interaction in a social order are very likely a powerful stabilizing influence in a social organization. That is, interaction relevant to different functional needs of actors compels the emergence of certain definite structural patterns among actors in the social organization. The impact of these media are especially important inasmuch as actors are probably unaware of their influence. For those interested in social change this is critical; for the very mode of interaction in a social order may be a stagnating influence in the system. Piecemeal alternation in the character of the nodes or in the rerouting of the flows of these resources may have only a minimal effect on the social order. It is still very likely that patterns of dominance and differentiation will be present with no real overall change resulting in the basic structuring of relationships.

Needless to say, our conclusions may be premature. A variety of social organizations need to be studied before we can make any definitive statements concerning the effects of different institutionalized media on interaction patterns. Our research is only a preliminary effort. Hopefully, through our discussion we can motivate other researchers to replicate our study, to describe the relative effects of these media in different types of relational systems, and to formulate more precise explanations of why these media affect interaction as they do.

NOTES

1. One problem in analyzing the centrality of organizations is that the researcher often assumes that there is one and only one "center" of a relational system and that actors are neatly arranged around this center. Certainly, we can think of structural systems where there is no center per se (i.e., all actors are equidistant to one another) and where there are multiple centers (see Mintz, 1978). This prompted us to look at the strong components within each of our asymmetric networks to see if either pattern was to be found. Our analysis showed us, however, that in each network there was only one large strong component with several individual organizations appended to it.

2. We characterize our hypotheses as "descriptive" rather than "causal." The data we have is for one time period only and thus we can only describe what we find at that particular time. A truly causal analysis is certainly possible, given longitudinal data; and we expect that many of our descriptive hypotheses can be translated into causal propositions. In this study, however, we must limit ourselves to only descriptive statements.

3. In Chapter 1 we argued that all organizations need money, information, and moral support in order to meet certain functional needs of theirs. In these hypotheses we are only suggesting that some organizations will probably have greater need for some of the resources due to the specific tasks and activities that they are engaged in.

4. A centrality score (C_i) for each actor for each asymmetric path distance matrix was computed using the following formula:

$$C_i = \frac{\sum\limits_{j=1}^{n} d_{ij} + \sum\limits_{j=1}^{n} d_{ji}}{2(n-1)}$$

where d_{ij} is the path distance from organizations i to j, d_{ji} is the path distance from organizations j to i, and n is equal to the number of organizations in the population. Diagonals (distances from actors to themselves) were not included in the computations.

5. There were three organizations that refused to provide this information. A fourth organization, the state university, said that it was impossible to know since payment comes through state taxes. Upon consultation with community informants, we assigned a value of .9% for this variable to the university.

6. The number of local employees and local members were all added up together for this variable.

7. These data were the most difficult to recover. Most organizations had budgets, and for these organizations we simply multiplied the budget (see Appendix C, Q5) by the percentage of funds that the organization spent in the local county (see Appendix C, Q9). For a number of other organizations, more indirect measures were needed. For example, for industries we multiplied the total sales for a corporation (see Appendix C, Q6) by the percent of funds that the entire corporation spent locally (Appendix C, Q9). For financial institutions, we used data provided by the Federal Reserve Bank of Illinois and the Federal Home Loan Bank of Chicago, who told us for 1973 how much money each of these organizations spent on local operations and how much interest each paid its depositors. These amounts were added together for our analyses. Finally, we needed figures for the three law firms. For this figure we used the simple formula:

Funds = (Mean income for attorneys) * (No. of attorneys in firm) + (Mean income for secretaries) * (No. of secretaries in firm) + (Rent and overhead)

= ($30,000) * ($N_A$) + ($9,000) * (N_S) + ($15,000)

The income figures were obtained from the U.S. Census of Occupations, 1970. The estimate for rent and overhead was given by a local informant.

8. All the industries, financial institutions, and law firms refused to answer this item, because there was no way for them to give exact figures. Rather than lose these organizations in our subsequent analyses, all the industries and law firms were assigned a value of 0.0%, and all financial institutions were given 5.0%. Considering how we recoded this variable we believe that no error was introduced by these assignments.

9. The county housing authority gets all of its funds from its clients. The city hospital receives all of its funds from patient fees, health insurance, and a private foundation. The hospital receives no money from the city, and is tied to city government only through administrative channels.

10. The identification of these roles was based on the following formula: A ratio coefficient, r_i, was computed for each of 20 subgroups of organizations for each medium.

$$r_i = \frac{\left(\sum_{j=1}^{n} v_{ji} \,/\, \sum_{j=1}^{n} v_{ij} \right) - 1}{\left(\sum_{j=1}^{n} v_{ji} \,/\, \sum_{j=1}^{n} v_{ij} \right) + 1}$$

$\sum_{j=1}^{n} v_{ji}$ is the total number of actors from which members of subgroup i received a particular resource, $\sum_{j=1}^{n} v_{ij}$ is the total number of actors to which members of subgroup i gave a particular resource, n is the total number of organizations in the population, and i goes from 1 to 20. Subgroups which had more outflows than inflows (generators) had negative ratio coefficients with a limit of −1.00. Subgroups which had more inflows than outflows (consumers) had positive scores with a limit of +1.00. A score of "zero" occurred if the number of inflows equaled the number of outflows. In identifying roles for subgroups, we decided that subgroups with scores of −1.00 to −0.33 were to be considered generators, −0.32 to +0.32 transmitters, and +0.33 to +1.00 consumers. In other words, to be classified as a generator (or consumer), the ratio of outflows to inflows (or inflows to outflows) had to be at least two to one.

The author would like to thank Peter Marsden for suggesting this measure to me.

11. For all correlations and regression analyses presented in Tables 3.4 and 3.5 involving MONEY, INFOR, or SUPPORT, we reversed the signs to make the tables easier to interpret. The reader will recall that these variables had originally been coded so that a lower score indicated that an actor was more central in a network, while a higher score indicated that an actor was more peripheral.

12. We omitted statistical tests of significance for R_2 and the Beta coefficients, since we are not dealing with a sample but a population of actors.

13. There were several reasons why we could only include 60 organizations in this analysis. First, six organizations had to be dropped because their agents had refused to respond to the items on social values. Second, six organizations had to be omitted because their agents were respondents for two organizations. Finally, we dropped the city council since we could not determine which of the six councilmen interviewed was the primary agent.

14. We had to use a three-dimensional solution for the value space since the coefficient of alienation for the two-dimensional solution was unacceptably high. The coefficient for the three-dimensional solution was .126.

Chapter 4

ORGANIZATIONAL ACTIVATION ON FIVE COMMUNITY ISSUES

So far we have argued that networks of money, information, and support flows among local formal organizations constitute three key social structures in the urban community. We described the social organization of these network structures by examining the relative positioning of organizations within each of them. It was apparent that organizations which had a greater economic interest in the community and which had more funds available to them were more central in each network. On the other hand, organizational proximity in the networks was based on a number of different factors including the auspices of the organizations, organizations' activities, and leadership values. In this chapter and the next, we examine how organizations' structural positions in these three networks affected their participation in different community issues.

A Theory of Community Conflict

The study of community decision-making has a long and stormy history both in sociology and political science. Supposedly, the debate between the "elitists" and "pluralists" has finally been laid to rest with the emergence of comparative studies. The advantage of comparative analyses is that they can evaluate the impact of different city-level structural variables on the centralization/ decentralization of political decision-making and the output of different services (see Aiken and Alford, 1970; Clark, 1971, 1972; Turk, 1970, 1973a, 1973b, 1977; Hawley, 1963; Lincoln, 1976; Smith, 1976; Liebert, 1976; Grimes et al., 1976). In a way, then, the case study presented here is a regression to a more "primitive" mode of analysis. However, we believe that there are some new wrinkles to the elitist/pluralist debate still to be explored and that new insights can be gained only through a close examination of the various institutional structures that community actors are involved in.

In contrast to earlier case studies, we do not focus as much on the fates and fortunes of individual interest groups as on relational subsystems that are functionally important for satisfying different needs of community actors, i.e., networks of money, information, and support flows. From our point of view, the political process is less a struggle between organizations for power and more an adaptive accommodation of existing institutional arrangements to demands for goods and services made in the community environ- ment.[1] Nevertheless, conflict is still an important part of the political process. Organizations compete to get into different posi- tions in the institutions themselves, and when institutional change comes, it often threatens actors' positions in the institutions. Our position is simply that to identify which actors get involved in community conflict, we ought to look at the roles different corporate actors play in community institutions rather than the interests and resources of the organizations themselves.

To approach community decision-making from an "institu- tional" perspective and to focus on the role of organizations in community institutions is certainly nothing new. For example, Banfield's (1961) study of political decision-making in Chicago focused on how the fates of different organizations were affected by the public policies which local social, political, and economic institutions were charged to implement. Individuals and organiza- tions were drawn into issues as demands were made on different

institutional structures to change in order to provide better services. The power of any one actor was a function of his occupying
a key position in the institution. Using a much different research
strategy, Turk (1973a) argued that the ability of a social system to
react to different demands placed upon it is dependent upon the
available linkages within and between different institutional sectors of the community. The existing structure of interorganizational linkages will either facilitate an immediate, innovative
response to demands for change or impede efforts to make local
institutions more responsive to local needs. A common theme that
runs through both of these studies and mine is that to understand
patterns of community decision-making, research must focus on
organizations as they are embedded in complex community institutions.

MARKETS, DEMANDS, AND POLITICAL CONFLICTS

What brings about community conflict and how can an "institutional" approach provide an answer that could explain how conflict is resolved and decisions are made? Summarized briefly,
decision-making structures or action sets emerge when institutionalized service structures are no longer able to satisfy local demands
for collective outputs of goods, services, or "leadership."

In the modern community demands are typically first articulated by discontented interest groups, which initiate action on their
own or in response to certain actions of governmental or corporate
bureaucracies. The research on community organization efforts in
city neighborhoods provides one example of this type of action
(e.g., Molotch, 1972; Fish, 1973; Rossi and Dentler, 1961).
Typically, activists focus their attention on the organizational
units which perform certain functions in the community and
demand that these "institutions" make some response to their
demands. For example, if neighborhood residents are upset about
the way that their children are being educated, they attack the
local school principal. As discontent over the provision of services
becomes greater, activists challenge not only the local school, but
also the very system by which legitimacy is conferred on actors
who are supposed to carry out socialization functions in the

community. For this reason, the action set which must respond to the protests includes not only the organization immediately involved in an issue but all those actors which are principally involved in conferring legitimacy upon that actor.[2]

Most of the time demands made by interest groups are easily met by agents working through these systems. Demands for various goods and services change over time; but organizational elites are expected to anticipate new market conditions and be flexible enough to change their policies accordingly.

At times, however, institutions cannot readily meet the demands made upon them. Abrupt changes in the local community or in the larger society may create demands that existing institutional arrangements simply cannot meet (e.g., the in-migration of a new ethnic/racial group or the decision to build a highway through a community). At this point various interests in the community have a legitimate "claim" against the ruling elites which dominate the respective institutions and can challenge their authority.[3] Subsequently, community conflict erupts between those who seek the change and those who occupy positions of control in the institutions (see Coleman, 1957; Turk, 1977; Gamson, 1968). If challengers have adequate resources and can discredit the institutional order, they may be able to wrest control of different institutional sectors from elites and install themselves into dominant positions. This action may be motivated not only to satisfy their own consumer needs but to also improve their own power in the system. More typically, elites in the institutions will seek either to coopt their critics or to find some way to alter the structure so as to appease the discontents.

It is in response to the discontents that collective decision-making structures or action sets arise within different institutional sectors. Some sort of ad hoc structure emerges either to reconcile the differences between the challengers and the agents of the established social order or to adjust or change social structures so as to meet the demands. Although the composition of these action sets may be affected by the resources and interests of different actors in the community, it is our thesis that the position, and specifically the centrality, of organizations in selected interorganizational networks will have a greater effect on the composition of these community decision-making structures.

INTERORGANIZATIONAL NETWORKS AND PATTERNS OF ORGANIZATIONAL ACTIVATION

In Chapter 1 we argued that community interorganizational resource networks of money, information, and support constitute key community structures relevant to different functional needs of community actors. Because organizations need to satisfy their own adaptive, problem-solving, and legitimacy needs, they enter into interorganizational relationships of money, information, and moral support. These dyadic linkages give rise to social networks that, in turn, define the perimeters of interaction in the community relevant to the satisfaction of these functional needs.

Because these networks are important institutional structures, we expect that an organization's position in these networks will affect its chances of participating in different decision-making action sets. As different community institutions are challenged, we expect that an actor's centrality in the interorganizational networks of money, information, and support will affect his chances of being activated by the challenge.

H11: The more central organizations are in money and in information networks, the more likely they will be activated on instrumental issues.

H12: The more central organizations are in support and in information networks, the more likely they will be activated on expressive issues.

As demands are made upon community institutions to change, we expect that those actors who are most responsible for the maintenance of those institutions and who have the greatest control over them will be drawn into the controversy. Since actors in the center of money, information, and support networks are clearly the most dominant actors in certain key functional institutions, we expect that they would be the ones to become active in different community issues. To begin with, actors in the centers of these systems have an extra special interest in becoming active, since they may lose their power and control in the network if they remain passive. Furthermore, these actors have a certain responsibility to the community and are seen as "natural leaders" by more peripheral actors in the network. Their minimal social distance to others in the system is an important asset in establishing a problem-solving action set. In addition, peripheral actors do have some recourse if dominents betray them. Although it may be somewhat costly, they can always weaken dominants' positions in the resource network by avoiding them or discriminating against them in their day-to-day interaction.

Our hypotheses state that centrality in different institutional structures will be more or less important in explaining activation as different issues develop, i.e., as different institutions are challenged. This, however, assumes that we have a clear understanding of the way in which issues differ and what types of issues are relevant for different functional sectors of community life (see Barth and Johnson, 1959; Clark, 1968; Freeman, 1968; Laumann and Pappi, 1976). Here we will classify issues into two general types: instrumental issues and expressive issues.

Laumann and Pappi (1973:224) argue that "instrumental issues are concerned with controversies over the differing allocation of scarce resources, such as land, jobs, and money and find their particular focus in the adaptive and integrative sectors of the community." Instrumental issues also involve the allocation of material rewards to different competing interest groups in a community. In this respect, instrumental issues are controversies over the distribution of private goods among actors in a system (see Clark, 1973a; 1973b:60-61). Here outgroups challenge legitimate institutions on the grounds that certain policies or practices effectively discriminate against them and in favor of another constituency.

Laumann and Pappi further argue that "expressive issues are concerned with controversies regarding the maintenance or change in the organization of basic values, commitments, and/or orientations that shall guide or control community affairs." This type of issue is centered more in the pattern maintenance and goal-attainment subsectors of the community. Not only do these issues involve the organization of values, but more importantly, they usually have implications for the allocation of public funds and what type of "public goods" or projects the community as a whole should sponsor. Here challengers to established institutions argue that authorities are no longer pursuing policies in harmony with the general wishes of the collectivity. Some challenges may question the very legitimacy of the institutional elites. It is understandable, then, that these issues "are usually highly charged with emotional affect and have an 'all or none' nature that usually precludes or makes very difficult negotiated settlements among the contending parties."

Needless to say, an issue can be redefined in the course of its resolution. If actors can control the "meaning" of an issue, they can often effectively control the level of controversy and the manner in which it is resolved (Schattschneider, 1960). For example, Coleman (1957) and Gamson (1966a) showed that once fluoridation had been redefined as being relevant to "national security," i.e., as an expressive issue, it was inevitably defeated. Therefore, we must be careful not to classify issues as being categorically one type of another.

Because instrumental issues are closely linked to adaptive processes and expressive issues are important for the identification of collective goals and symbols, we expect that organizations which occupy central positions in the money network are more likely to be activated on instrumental issues, while centrality in the support network will influence the activation of organizations on expressive issues. Centrality in the information network, because this network is important for problem-solving in general, will be important on all types of issues.

> H13: Organizations' funds, size, dependency on the local community for funds, and headquarters' location will have an indirect effect on their participation in community decision-making. The effects of these variables will be mediated by organizations' centrality in the money, information, and support networks. Organizations' activities, however, will have a direct effect on their participation.

Pluralists have been writing about political resources and their use in collective decision-making for sometime now. French and

Raven (1959), Dahl (1971), Laumann and Pappi (1976), Gamson (1966b), Clark (1968), and Coleman (1971) have discussed the use of a wide range of resources in different decision-making contexts. Particular attention is given to when certain resources are more or less effective. To protect their self-interests, actors must not only control enough resources, but, more importantly, highly generalizable resources. Actors who control more resources which other actors need (e.g., money and popular support) have the advantage of being able to become active in more decision-making situations than those who have less resources.

Pluralists have also argued that an organizations' interests will influence their participation in community decision-making. An important factor which often defines an actor's interests is its source of funding and legitimacy. Very simply, organizations which are less dependent on extralocal systems and more dependent on local systems for their survival will be more interested in local community decision-making and will subsequently become more involved in local issues (Clark, 1968:50-51, 1973b:50; Walton, 1967; Warren, 1956, 1963; Levine and White, 1961; Schulze, 1961). Beginning with the work of Warner, this hypothesis has received a great deal of attention and has been important in explaining the declining participation of economic actors in local community affairs.

The activities or functions of organizations should also be important in explaining activation patterns. Pluralists also argue that organizations whose mandated function is to engage in community problem-solving activities (e.g., public decision-making bodies) are more likely to become active in community issues. Indeed, this proposition may seem almost commonsensical; however, it does acknowledge that certain actors in a community are recognized as legitimate arbiters in conflict situations. For our analysis its inclusion is important, for it helps us to assess the effects of organizations' resources, interests, and centrality on participation in community decision-making coalitions independent of organizational domain.

We agree that problem-solving organizations will be active on all issues, but in contrast to the pluralists' position, our hypothesis argues that resources and dependencies will have an indirect rather than a direct effect on activation. The centrality of an organization in the different resource networks will be more important in explaining participation. Indeed, we expect that resources and interests are important in attaining positions of dominance or centrality in the respective networks, as was suggested in our findings in Chapter 3. But we expect that the direct effect of these variables on organizational activation will be relatively weak. Rather than the individual resources and interests of the organizations, it will be the position of organizations in different community institutional networks that will be important in explaining activation on different issues.

Operationalization of the Variables

Most of the variables for this analysis are already familiar to the reader. For organizations' resources, we used an organization's control over funds (FUNDS) and its control over personnel (PERS); for its interests in the local community, we used percentage of its cash inflow from local sources (INFL) and whether it had its headquarters located in the community (HDQTLOC). To determine whether organizations were functionally responsible for decision-making and conflict resolution, we used the three-fold classification of economic (ECON), problem-solving (PROBLEM), and service organizations (SERVICE). Organizations were classified either as problem-solving or not for this analysis. Measures of organizations' centrality in the money network (MONEY), the information network (INFOR), and the support network (SUPPORT) were again organizations' centrality scores for the respective SSA-I solutions. Since the construction and recoding of all these variables were discussed in Chapter 3, we will not comment any further on them here.

We also measured organizations' activation in five community issues.[4] There were many different ways that we could have done this; the method we used seemed to us the simplest. We first identified five community issues that could be examined in some detail. Rather than taking a random sample of issues, we wanted issues which were nontrivial and which were representative of different types of controversies in the community. In preliminary interviews, we asked eight positional leaders to recall and describe some of the most important issues in Towertown between 1970 and 1974.[5] From these interviews and our review of local newspapers, we decided on four actual issues and one hypothetical issue. The five issues are listed below:

(A) the closing of a laboratory school by the board of education;
(B) the imposition of a curfew after university student disturbances;
(C) the construction of a community health services center;
(D) the relocation of a new post office;
(E) the jurisdiction of city versus county officials over a new regional airport (hypothetical).

The next task was to identify the organizations in the community that became involved in each issue. There were three ways in which these data were gathered. First, we examined newspaper

Table 4.1:   Frequency Distribution for Activation on Five Community Issues

Issue		Value	Frequency	Percentage
School	Not active	0	64	87.7
	Active	1	9	12.3
	Mean	.12		
	Standard deviation	.33		
Curfew	Not active	0	64	86.3
	Active	1	10	13.7
	Mean	.14		
	Standard deviation	.35		
Hospital	Not active	0	41	56.2
	Active	1	32	43.8
	Mean	.44		
	Standard deviation	.50		
Post office	Not active	0	62	84.9
	Active	1	11	15.1
	Mean	.15		
	Standard deviation	.36		
Airport	Not active	0	63	86.3
	Active	1	10	13.7
	Mean	.14		
	Standard deviation	.35		

accounts of these issues; then we asked respondents if their organization became involved in an issue (see Appendix C, Q15); and, finally, we asked members of the "community elite" to identify those organizations in the community which they thought were active on the different issues (or would be active in the case of the hypothetical issue).[6] For the analyses below, we use only the set of "activists" generated through the last method, although the other methods were used to check on the accuracy of our information.[7] An organization was considered active on an issue if at least one of the community elite said that the organization was active on that issue (SCHL, CURF, HOSP, PO, AIRP). The frequency distribution for activation on each issue is presented in Table 4.1 along with means and standard deviations.

Synopsis of Community Issues

The crux of our analysis is to see if organizations which were more central in different interorganizational networks were also active in different community issues. This, of course, implies that we can classify our issues either as instrumental or expressive. Needless to say, no issue is exclusively one type or another; elements of both ideal types can be found in all five issues. Our strategy will be to review in detail all the issues and then classify them according to the more pervasive definitions of the issues by community actors.[8]

THE POST OFFICE ISSUE

As happened in many middle-size communities, in the 1960s the availability of federal funds for urban renewal efforts touched off a flurry of political activity in Towertown. One of this town's more interesting confrontations over the past decade took place over the relocation and construction of a new, federally funded post office in the downtown area.

In the late 1960s the U.S. Post Office in Washington sent word to the town's postmaster that there would be federal funds available to build a new post office in Towertown. The postmaster was to work closely with city officials in identifying a site for the new building and then to submit a proposal to Washington for final approval. The business community, city officials, and most community residents supported the project. At this time, the mayor enjoyed considerable support from the business community.

A site was finally chosen by city officials and the postmaster on the west end of the downtown area in the middle of the retail and banking district. This area was chosen because of its central location for shoppers and its proximity to the university. Needless to say, the businessmen who owned the land on which the post office was to be built and the adjacent properties were most pleased.

Before the plans were finalized, however, there was a mayoral election in 1969 and the business-supported incumbent lost. The new mayor had a much different constituency and a different set of priorities. Drawing support from agricultural interests, the working classes, and older established families, he embodied a growing discontent with the "business-dominated" city administration. To no one's surprise, one of the first moves of the new administration was to tear up the plans for the west end location of the post office and to begin a new search for a more "suitable site."

The new administration proposed that the location for the post office should be on the east end of the business district which was an area of small, specialty shops. The administration's argument for this site was that this was a great opportunity to rejuvenate a struggling section of the central business district. By bringing more traffic into the area, the businesses there would get a new lease on life.

The revised proposal was drawn up by city officials and the postmaster and sent to Washington for approval. This action, however, was not well received by the businessmen on the west side. Meetings were held, letters were sent to Washington, and charges of graft and corruption were leveled at city officials. At one point a number of businessmen stormed into the city manager's office, demanded his resignation, and threatened to "fire" the city council. All of this commotion only made the city officials more resolute in their decision and had the unanticipated effect of rallying the city council and the townspeople behind the city officials. After a while the controversy finally died down, Washington accepted the new site, and the new post office was eventually built on the east end of the central business district.

The second issue involved a citywide curfew that was imposed by the mayor of Towertown following violent student disturbances in May of 1970. These events happened in the wake of demonstrations by university students against the United States invasion of Cambodia and the Kent State-Jackson State student killings.

The demonstration that led to the curfew began as a peaceful march from the university campus to the central business district. When the demonstrators reached the downtown area, about 150 students broke ranks and began smashing windows in several of the stores. Subsequently, the police attacked the rioting students and drove the rioters and demonstrators out of the downtown area across a small bridge which separated the university from the rest of the town. At this point students and police squared off.

Actions by university administrators and the police themselves, however, helped to avert further violence. Seeing the situation deteriorate, a number of administrators hurried down to the bridge in hopes of preventing a violent confrontation. The president of the university, wearing a baseball cap, mingled with the students trying to calm them down. At the same time, the police, nose-to-nose with the students, were shielding the students from the irate townspeople coming out of the town. Many residents had come out of their homes with chains and baseball bats to help the police suppress the disturbance.

In the wake of these events, the mayor and city manager thought it would be in the best interest of the community to impose a curfew on the city until tensions eased. There was only one problem. The mayor had no legal power to issue such an order without the city council's approval. The mayor decided to issue the "illegal" order anyway, and the city police complied.

Although everyone in the community agreed that something had to be done to restore order; many individuals and groups from different sectors of the community questioned the methods of the city officials. Some charged that the curfew was too severe, inconveniencing a number of innocent young people; other opposed its illegality. Still others thought that the city was too lenient. Some members of the county board even suggested that the city immediately file suit against the university for damages to the businesses and for the costs of imposing the curfew. The debate over the curfew, however, did not last long since the action effectively stopped the violence.

THE SCHOOL ISSUE

This issue actually began to develop in 1971 two years before the confrontation between school officials and parents. At that time the school, Garvey (pseudonym), was a part of the university's school of education. It was an experimental school housed in a university building, run by university staff and students, and attended by about 350 children. Because of the location of the school, the overwhelming majority of these students were children of university faculty and staff and of professionals in the community. The problems for Garvey began when the state cut the general budget of the university, and the university administration, in turn, decided to eliminate the lab school program.

The program at Garvey, however, was not to be terminated immediately. In an effort to save the school, the board of education had come to an agreement with the university that the board would administer the program at Garvey, provide the staff, and retain a curriculum similar to the one that had been there previously. In two years, the board of education would close the school, but by that time a new school would have been built by the district to service the students now at Garvey. It was the understanding of the parents that the Garvey program would be adopted at the new school.

As the time for Garvey's closing drew near, the school board was petitioned by Garvey parents either to keep the school open or, at least, to guarantee that its program would be adopted in the new school. The board reaffirmed its position that Garvey would be closed but made no guarantees that the program would be transferred to the new school. The board had reevaluated the curriculum at Garvey and recommended that the new school should have a traditional curriculum just like every other elementary school in the district.

The decision sparked a vehement protest from parents at Garvey. They felt that the city had reneged on its commitment to "progressive" education and had succumbed to outside pressures in the community. At this point, other actors in the community joined the fray in support of the board. Many objected to having a school which served primarily upper middle class children and which had special privileges and special programs that the whole community would be paying for. That the school would have an open enrollment policy made little difference, since the district had no bus system and students from other parts of town would have to incur unreasonable transportation costs to get there.

In the end, the board held to its policy that Garvey would be closed, but it did concede that certain "progressive" programs would be started at the new school as well as in all the other elementary schools in the district. This seemed to pacify the parents; however, many felt that ultimately their interests might be best served by convincing university administrators to reopen a lab school under the sponsorship of the university.

THE AIRPORT ISSUE

The debate over the construction of a new airport in this community has a long history. As far back as 1965, the mayor, supported by a number of businessmen, recommended that the city build a new airport. Financing with the federal government was arranged, and plans for purchasing the land were made. The city administrators had even arranged to sell some property that the city owned to pay the city's share of the costs thus making new taxes unnecessary. All that was needed was the approval of the city council for the final plans. The council vote, however, was not taken until after the 1969 city elections; and it was in this election that a strong working class and conservative coalition replaced the incumbents, who were closely tied to the business community. Needless to say, the airport, labeled as a "middle class folly," was soundly defeated by the new council.

The prospects of building a new airport remained dormant for a number of years. Because of its latency, we thought that this would have been a good hypothetical issue, and we included it in our interview schedule as such. However, after we had been interviewing for about a month, the issue reemerged, and the controversey raged once again.

The circumstances surrounding the reemergence of this issue are quite interesting. A few years prior to our fieldwork, the state tollway authority had built a superhighway running east-west along the southern edge of Towertown. As part of the original plan, a four-lane extension road was to be built extending northward from the highway along the east end of Towertown in order to link communities in the northern end of the county with the highway. Everyone favored the construction of this road: a great deal of traffic would be diverted away from the town, industrial parks could be built along the extension road at some distance from residential areas, and neither the city nor the county would have to pay for it.

The county board was to have the responsibility for planning and building the extension road. Following normal procedures, the board appointed a committee to make recommendations for the exact location of the road together with contingency plans. Interestingly enough, the committee recommended that the cheapest and most efficient route for the new road would run right through the old airport located on the east end of town. If this plan was adopted, it would mean that a new airport would have to be built.

Although we expected that the old opponents to a new airport would come out strongly against the committee's recommendation, this did not happen. The only question raised was who was going to pay for a new airport—the city or the county.

At the completion of our fieldwork, it was still not clear who was going to "win" or "lose" this round. The county board adopted both the committee's recommendations and a strongly worded resolution that the county board would have nothing to do with the construction of a new airport. It seemed that the farmers in the southern part of the county were determined that they would not pay for an airport that only the businessmen in Towertown would enjoy.

THE HEALTH SERVICES CENTER ISSUE

The final issue involved the construction of a new health services center in the community. This issue was perhaps the most controversial of all.

The idea for a new health services center originated in the board room of the old city hospital. In 1969, a series of studies were conducted, sponsored by the hospital's board of directors, to determine population patterns in future years. The findings of these studies suggested that if population trends continued, more health services would be needed and new facilities would have to be built. In response to this recommendation, a nonprofit corporation under the auspices of the hospital board was formed in 1970 to explore the idea of building a new, comprehensive, health care facility.

At first, there was strong support for the project in the community. Individuals and organizations from the business community were especially enthusiastic. The manpower for promotions and fund raising came primarily from this sector. Over time the project became more and more identified solely with business interests.

About one year after the project began, strong opposition surfaced. First, there were serious objections from old, established families as well as from working class segments of the population who were virtually excluded from the planning of the project. At that time, these groups were represented in the city council, and thus most of the vocal opposition came from the council and other city administrators. The opposition's arguments focused on the increased cost for the community as a whole, the adequacy of the current hospital, and the inconvenient location of the proposed site (patients would need an automobile to reach it). While some of these arguments were well taken, this opposition seemed to have had other motives. One of the most important was that the city hospital had great symbolic meaning for many old-time residents. All of the financial support for the old hospital had come from private local foundations set up decades ago by the town's earliest families.

Second, a group of general practitioners also opposed the new health facility. The doctors argued that there were enough specialized services in the nearby metropolis and that their own practices would be jeopardized by the new center. Some observers, however, felt that much of the opposition in the medical profession was due to the fact that the new administrators for the health services center were wary of letting local physicians gain too much control of the new center and, at first, did not even offer office space to the doctors.

Between 1970 and 1972, no one was really quite sure if a new health services center would be built because of the opposition to the project. After 1972, however, there was a number of developments that turned the tide in favor of those who supported the new health center.

First, the proponents of the hospital were able to tap new financial resources that enabled them to build the facility without the support of local tax dollars. On the local level, there were substantial contributions from two large private organizations: A farm association and a locally owned industrial firm. The latter's contribution was especially significant. The family who owned the business had long been associated with the community and had a firm commitment to the area's continued growth.

These contributions, however, sparked still another series of controversies. The industrial firm wanted to maintain a low profile, and thus discreetly negotiated its gift with the center's administrators. When the news of the contribution leaked out, a number of townspeople were incensed and charged collusion on the part of hospital officials. At the same time, there were accusations that the executives of the farm association had committed a $1 million dollar pledge without consulting its membership. Although there was nothing underhanded or illegal about either organization's actions, it was apparent that they had handled their public relations poorly and generated much suspicion in the community.

The health center's administrators also were successful in securing funds from outside public sources. The state department of
public health, for example, made available over one million dollars
for mental health programs. The allocation of these funds, though,
also generated considerable controversy, since a local mental
health board was finally charged with the responsibility to decide
whether or not these funds should go to the new center or to
existing programs. There was still more controversy when the new
center began eyeing county funds and the consolidation of all
county service agencies in their facility.

Finally, changes in the city administration as a result of the
1973 city elections proved to be most important of all for the
construction of the center. Both the proponents and opponents of
the center sponsored candidates in the aldermanic and mayoral
races. Although a candidate opposing the new hospital was elected
mayor, the hospital's supporters secured two more seats in the
council giving them a majority. At this juncture, the mood of the
council radically changed, and measures favorable to the new
center were readily passed.

At the completion of our fieldwork in the winter of 1975,
ground for the new center had been broken and the center was
finally being built.

DISCUSSION

Even with these detailed accounts, it is still not immediately
apparent which issues are instrumental and which are expressive.
We would suggest that one way to categorize our issues is to
identify the "challengers" in the issues and to recount the arguments they made against the institutional elites involved in the
conflict. If challengers raised allegations that questioned the legitimacy or "good faith" of institutional elites, then we can type the
issue as expressive. On the other hand, if challengers charge that
institutions in their policies were being somehow "unfair" in
allocating scarce resources to them, then the issue can be typed as
instrumental.

Using these criteria, the school controversy was clearly an
expressive issue. The challengers were angry parents who charged

that school officials had betrayed a commitment to alternative educational forms. School officials replied that alternative education programs were no longer seen as "effective" and that traditional forms were more acceptable. The controversy became "rancorous" when other organizations and population subgroups in the community rallied behind the board and charged Garvey parents with elitism voicing resentment toward university faculty and staff who felt that their children were "too good" to share the same school facilities with the rest of the community.

The curfew issue similarly can be typed as an expressive issue. Here both liberals from the university community and local businessmen balked at the policies of the local officials, charging that officials had violated the trust of the people. The rationales for their position, of course, were quite different. Although there was the potential for a full-blown confrontation over the curfew decision, the issue never fully matured. The redeeming quality of the mayor's decision was that it worked. That the method violated values of different interests in the community was overshadowed by the fact that the common threat of violence had been removed.

Typing the hospital issue is more difficult, since it seems to have had both expressive and instrumental traits. In one way the issue was clearly expressive. Proponents of the hospital saw its construction as an important community project which symbolized the economic growth and development of Towertown. Opponents of the hospital argued that the new hospital would jeopardize the semirural atmosphere of the community, identify Towertown more with the metropolitan community to the east, and close down the hospital which was one of the last remaining symbols of the old barb wire dynasties. On the other hand, the issue was also debated on instrumental grounds. Arguments over the duplication of services and the reallocation of funds from existing programs were common. In this respect, challengers to the hospital argued to protect their own self-interests, which they felt the new health service center would threaten.

The post office issue was more clearly an instrumental issue. In this conflict, downtown businessmen were the challengers. It seems that the decision by city officials to relocate the post office in the east end of the central business district was perceived by merchants and bankers as an unfair attack on their economic well-being. A "bureaucratic" decision had been originally made in their favor, yet it was overturned by a "political" decision of the new administration.

Finally, the airport seemed to be the most instrumental issue of all. As the issue was formulated by us, the controversy revolved around control over the new facility. Here the parties challenging one another were two institutional structures which had a vested interest in not taking responsibility for the airport. We had anticipated that the city council and the county board each feared the disapproval of its respective constituency and thus would seek to transfer control of the airport to the other party. As this was a hypothetical issue, we obviously do not know the type of argument each actor would evoke; however, when asked, we said that mostly legal and technical arguments would be put forth in defense of each actor's interests.

Analysis of Organizational Activation on Five Community Issues

In the following paragraphs we will present five path models describing which organizations became active on each of the five issues. For all our models we will assume that there is a weak causal ordering among our variables and that the exogenous variables are not causally related. Furthermore, we will assume that all our relationships are linear.[9] Again we will not estimate population parameters nor specify levels of statistical significance for Beta coefficients since we are still looking at a population of actors. For each model we will evaluate the total effects, direct effects (path coefficients), and indirect effects of each of our explanatory variables. We will begin by analyzing the more expressive issues and then move on to the more instrumental issues.

We would suggest that the reader interpret the regression equations with some care. Since our study is limited to one time period, our results are descriptive rather than explanatory. This is especially important to keep in mind since some of the issues were actually settled three years before we even went into the field. Thus we are "predicting" activation on issues that were resolved in the early 1970s with data on organizations gathered in 1973. This applies to data on organizations' resources and interests as well as to data on centrality in the resource networks. Consequently, we can proceed with our analysis only if we assume that organizations and the networks among them are stable over a four or five year period and that the networks and the distribution of resources among organizations that we found in 1973 were not influenced by the way that the different issues were resolved in the earlier years.

Before we examine the path models we might want to look at the intercorrelation matrix for our five dependent variables. This matrix is presented in Table 4.2. It is important to examine the intercorrelations, because we may find similar patterns in our path models simply because the same organizations are active on the same issues. We see that for the most part activation on one issue is not related to activation on another. Among our four "real" issues the only high correlation is between activation on the curfew (CURF) and the post office (PO) issues. The relatively high correlations between activation on the airport issue (AIRP) and the other activation variables are understandable, since for hypothetical issues respondents are likely to identify potential participants on the basis of who has been participating in other issues. As we might expect, our panel of experts suggested that organizations involved in the town's more instrumental issues would be active on this instrumental issue as well.

Table 4.2: Means, Ranges, Standard Deviations, and the Intercorrelation Matrix of the Five Activation Variables

	SCHL	CURF	HOSP	PO	AIRP	Mean	Standard Deviation	Range
SCHL	1.000					.123	.331	0−1
CURF	.093	1.000				.137	.346	0−1
HOSP	.256	.049	1.000			.438	.499	0−1
PO	.191	.500	.245	1.000		.151	.360	0−1
AIRP	.214	.305	.451	.389	1.000	.137	.346	0−1

SCHOOL ISSUE

The first issue to be examined is the school controversy. Looking at the effects of our centrality variables on activation (see Table 4.3), we see immediately that SUPPORT had the strongest positive direct effect.[10] Organizations which were more central in the support network were more likely to be activated on this issue. Since the school issue was an expressive issue, we had expected this. Centrality in the information network (INFOR) had the second strongest effect among the network variables. This also was expected, since actors central in information networks are more likely to be activated on all issues.

We had hypothesized that organizational resources would have no direct effect on SCHL and a positive indirect effect. We see that while FUNDS does have a positive indirect effect, it also has a strong negative direct effect, i.e., the wealthier an organization, the less likely its activation. Although "poorer" organizations tended to get directly involved in this issue, the positive indirect effect of FUNDS suggests that financial resources were useful in enabling organizations to establish themselves in dominant interorganizational positions, which, in turn, gave them access to coalitions. In contrast, PERS had a weak positive direct effect on activation but no indirect effect. The sheer size of an organization seems to have had some direct impact on its participation. Perhaps

Table 4.3: Activation on the School Issue

Dependent Variable	Predictor Variables	Original Covariation	Direct Effect	Indirect Effect	Total Effect
SCHL	FUNDS	-.122	-.353	.359	.006
	PERS	.217	.143	.064	.207
	INFL	.108	-.260	.234	-.026
	HDQTLOC	-.206	-.268	.131	-.137
	PROBLEM	.276	.325	-.003	.322
	MONEY	.129	.065	–	.065
	INFOR	.255	.191	–	.191
	SUPPORT	.225	.335	–	.335

R =
R Square =

in expressive issues the more "citizen" support an organization can muster, the better able it is to penetrate decision-making action sets (Gamson, 1966a; Coleman, 1957). Organizations' interests were also expected to have only indirect effects on activation. However, HDQTLOC and INFL have negative direct effects on activation along with their positive indirect effects. Since the issue pitted "locals" against "cosmopolitans," the explanation of these findings might be quite simple. On the one hand, locals became active in this issue by virtue of their position in local resource networks which they dominated. Being central in the support network was especially important in predicting activation, and local actors were more central in this network. On the other hand, the activation of outsiders is reflected in the strong negative direct effects of INFL and HDQTLOC. Actors who typically would be uninterested in community affairs because of their extralocal commitments were drawn into the controversy only after it was defined as an issue which pitted their "cosmopolitan" values against a "local" value system.

Finally, PROBLEM has an important direct effect on activation. Since this variable is an indicator of which organizations are responsible for community decision-making and conflict resolution, we had expected that it would have its own independent effect on SCHL. It is clear that community decision-making organizations, voluntary associations, and the mass media as a group were more active in this issue.

CURFEW ISSUE

Again looking first at our network variables, we see in Table 4.4 that only INFOR is an important network variable predicting activation. We had hypothesized that SUPPORT would be more important than it was because the curfew was an expressive issue. One possible explanation for the weak effect of SUPPORT is that the issue never fully matured. Subsequently the collective solidarity and the stability of the support structure may never have been seriously threatened. In our description of the events surrounding the curfew, we saw that decisions were made very quickly; and that the debate surrounding the curfew was cut off as soon as the immediate crisis passed.

It is quite understandable why centrality in the information network would be important for this issue. Since the rioters presented a threat to the law and order of the community, actors who had better access to fast-breaking developments would be activated to help restore social order. The remarkably strong effect of INFOR is a testimony to the importance of existing information networks in shaping a community's response to a crisis or disaster, for clearly it was the structure of this network that "selected" which organizations would assume leadership roles.

As we found in the school issue, FUNDS has a negative direct effect but a positive indirect effect on activation. Again, organizations with less funds were drawn directly into the controversy as it developed, while wealthier organizations were active by virtue of their being central in the interorganizational networks and particularly the information network. That organizations with fewer economic resources participate more in expressive issues may be quite common. The "all or nothing" character of these issues may activate a large number of actors who are otherwise marginal to community affairs and peripheral in community institutions. Finally, we find that PERS has almost no effect at all on activation in this case.

Table 4.4: Activation on the Curfew Issue

Dependent Variable	Predictor Variables	Original Covariation	Direct Effect	Indirect Effect	Total Effect
CURF	FUNDS	-.103	-.282	.254	-.028
	PERS	-.065	.061	.039	.100
	INFL	.134	-.109	.228	.119
	HDQTLOC	.242	.218	.090	.308
	PROBLEM	.223	.104	.065	.169
	MONEY	.030	-.073	—	-.073
	INFOR	.413	.582	—	.582
	SUPPORT	.163	-.106	—	-.106

R = .554
R Square = .307

Looking at the interest variables, we see that INFL has a positive indirect effect on CURF and a very weak direct effect, while HDQTLOC has a positive direct effect and almost no indirect effect. Our findings for INFL are consistent with our hypotheses. Organizations dependent on the local community tend to be more central in the interorganizational network structures, and it is through these institutionalized positions that they participate in community decisions. We did not anticipate the independent positive effect of HDQTLOC on CURF. Upon reflection, however, it does make some sense. In a riot situation damage to buildings and other physical structures is a major concern. In Towertown there was a great deal of stone throwing and window smashing, thus it is not surprising that local actors, e.g., business organizations and city services, would be involved in this issue. The weak indirect effect is less mysterious, since it is due to the weak relation between HDQTLOC and the centrality scores (see Chapter 3).

On this issue the direct effect of PROBLEM is less important than in the school controversy, though the direction of the relation is positive. Again, perhaps the quick resolution of the issue is critical here. It may be that there never was enough time for the proper authorities (e.g., the city council) to be given jurisdiction over the decision. As a result, position in the information network was much more critical and on that basis organizations assumed responsibility for restoring order.

HOSPITAL ISSUE

The third issue to be examined is the hospital issue. Looking at the network variables in Table 4.5, we see that this time both MONEY and SUPPORT have a positive direct effect on activation while INFOR has little effect at all. Since this issue is both instrumental and expressive, these findings are consistent with our hypotheses. Organizations in the center of the money network were important probably because capital was needed for the project; actors in the center of the support network were critical, probably because new cultural definitions of the hospital became necessary as it became a threat to the rural character of the community and the dominance of certain traditional community symbols. It is, however, surprising that centrality in the information network was insignificant in this model.

The behavior of FUNDS is also consistent with our hypotheses. While FUNDS has a strong indirect effect on HOSP, it has a weak direct effect. We might note that this is the first time that FUNDS has had a positive effect on an activation variable; its direct effect in the two previous issues has been negative. The need to generate vast amounts of private capital for the new health service center may have drawn in actors who had control over large amounts of economic resources. Furthermore, because this project had become the "pet" of the business community, we would expect that wealthy business organizations would be overrepresented in this issue. Looking at PERS we see that the number of people affiliated with an organization had almost no effect whatsoever on its activation.

The two interest variables behave somewhat erratically. First, we see that INFL has a negative direct effect on HOSP and a positive indirect effect. This pattern does not quite conform to our expectations but is consistent with INFL's behavior in the two previous expressive issue. This issue may very well have been defined by some as another "local" versus "cosmopolitan" issue. Those that supported the new health center certainly seemed to be more "progressive" in their attitudes toward the community, while more "old fashioned" types dominated the opposition. If so,

Table 4.5: Activation on the Hospital Issue

Dependent Variable	Predictor Variables	Original Covariation	Direct Effect	Indirect Effect	Total Effect
HOSP	FUNDS	.420	.185	.429	.614
	PERS	.170	.018	.061	.079
	INFL	-.214	-.162	.200	.038
	HDQTLOC	.097	-.053	.073	.020
	PROBLEM	.019	.313	.024	.337
	MONEY	.547	.368	–	.368
	INFOR	.337	.026	–	.026
	SUPPORT	.415	.217	–	.217

R = .631
R Square = .398

then we again see the "cosmopolitans" drawn in directly to an issue which threatened their values rather than their economic interests, while the "locals" participated more indirectly through their domination of local network structures. Also in line with earlier findings, the location of an organization's headquarters has almost no effect at all on its activation.

Finally, we see that organizations involved in general community problem solving are more active than those engaged in human services or the economy. This is also as we expected. We imagine that PROBLEM's strength in this model reflects the length of time that the issue was given to mature and to be allocated to the appropriate decision-making bodies for deliberation. This, of course, is in contrast to developments in the curfew issue.

POST OFFICE ISSUE

On this issue we had expected that centrality in the information and money networks would be important in explaining activation. Looking at Table 4.6, INFOR clearly has the strongest direct effect of the three centrality variables and, in fact, is the best predictor of activation in the model. It now has been important in three of the four issues studied. Looking at the development of the issue, it is not difficult to understand why INFOR is as strong as it is. The whole controversy was marked by a great deal of

Table 4.6: Activation on the Post Office Issue

Dependent Variable	Predictor Variables	Original Covariation	Direct Effect	Indirect Effect	Total Effect
PO	FUNDS	.032	-.102	.344	.242
	PERS	-.072	.025	.053	.078
	INFL	.158	.172	.232	.404
	HDQTLOC	.264	.280	.099	.379
	PROBLEM	.021	-.103	.038	-.065
	MONEY	.172	.090	–	.090
	INFOR	.362	.341	–	.341
	SUPPORT	.218	.100	–	.100

R = .459
R Square = .211

confusion, and the need for information on the part of participants would understandably draw actors dominant in information
systems into this issue. We had expected, however, that MONEY
would have had a stronger effect than it did. This issue involved
the reallocation of federal money for a project which affected the
economic growth and development of downtown businesses, yet
its effect is as strong as that of centrality in the support network
(SUPPORT).

Looking at the resource variables, as expected neither FUNDS
nor PERS have a strong positive direct effect on activation; and
FUNDS does have a significant indirect effect. Once again, the
amount of money that organizations control does not automati-
cally give them access to decision-making action sets; rather position in a relational system is more critical. That we should find
this in an issue such as the post office, which is clearly instrumental, is a testimony to the importance of these network structures in mediating the effectiveness of money as a resource.

The direct effects of INFL and HDQTLOC on this issue are
much stronger than in the other three issues. Having local headquarters is especially important. This is probably due to the fact
that this issue is again related to the use/abuse of downtown
property. The only other issue where HDQTLOC had a positive
direct effect was the curfew issue, which was also important to
downtown businesses. Needless to say, issues concerning local
property investments are distinctively "local" in nature and would
activate a disproportionately large number of local actors
(Molotch, 1976).

Finally, to our surprise, PROBLEM is weakly and negatively
related to activation. This finding is difficult to explain. The issue
matured fully, and there was a great deal of public debate surrounding it. Perhaps a disproportionate number of economic
actors became involved in this issue; even so, this finding is
somewhat curious.

AIRPORT ISSUE

Finally, let us examine activation on the airport issue. When we
look at Table 4.7, it is apparent that none of the centrality

variables have very much of an effect on AIRP. In fact, no Beta coefficient is greater than .08. On the other hand, the two resource variables, FUNDS and PERS, have strong direct effects on AIRP and weak indirect effects. Although INFL has no effect on activation, HDQTLOC and PROBLEM also have direct effects.

These findings obviously contradict our hypotheses, since organizations' resources and interests directly affect AIRP, while our network variables are quite weak. We must remember, however, that this issue is a hypothetical one. When identifying participants in this controversy, our panel of experts were really identifying those who they thought would participate and not those who actually did. It may be that the networks we are studying are so subtle that many of the elites did not know the structural positions of other organizations in the community. If so, we should not expect them to take the centrality of other actors into account when speculating on the possible participants in this issue.

It would also follow that the resource variables would have strong direct effects on activation. Because an organization's resources are more visible than its positions in these networks, respondents identified potential participants primarily on the basis of how much money they controlled or how many people were affiliated with them. Similar arguments can be made regarding the relative strength of HDQTLOC and PROBLEM. Organizations which have local roots and organizations responsible for resolving

Table 4.7: Activation on the Airport Issue

Dependent Variable	Predictor Variables	Original Covariation	Direct Effect	Indirect Effect	Total Effect
AIRP	FUNDS	.279	.277	.071	.348
	PERS	.280	.270	.011	.281
	INFL	-.122	.008	.047	.055
	HDQTLOC	.079	.102	.020	.122
	PROBLEM	.063	.262	.009	.271
	MONEY	.251	.022	–	.022
	INFOR	.228	.072	–	.072
	SUPPORT	.202	.015	–	.015

R = .451
R Square = .204

integrative problems in the community are more visible and thus were regarded as likely candidates to participate in the decision.

SUMMARY

In the paragraphs above we have examined the effects of centrality in the three networks of money, information, and support on participation in five community issues. Because we have presented a great deal of data, we will briefly summarize our findings below.

We hypothesized that the amount of resources organizations controlled would have weak direct effects on activation but positive indirect effects. Furthermore, these effects would be mediated by organizations' centrality in the money, information, and support networks. We found this generally to be true for all the "real" issues we looked at but not for the hypothetical issue.

In the school issue, the curfew issue, the post office issue, and the hospital issue, FUNDS had a negative or weak direct effect on activation and a strong positive indirect effect. These findings suggest that although money helped organizations gain access to dominant, central positions in the different network structures, it was because of these structural positions, and not because of the amount of funds controlled, that organizations participated in decision-making. In fact, on the more expressive issues wealthier actors tended to remain passive, while less wealthy actors became active. In these types of issues the direct use of money as an influence resource may have been tabooed, and so actors controlling large funds tended to stay out of the controversy. In fact, where FUNDS had a moderate positive direct effect on activation (the hospital issue), intense conflict broke out, feelings against moneyed interests ran high, and the project sponsors came under severe attack.

In contrast, PERS had a moderately strong direct effect on activation on the school and airport issues and very weak indirect effects in all our analyses. The weakness of this variable suggests that size may affect activation only in special cases.

We were also interested in evaluating the effects of organizations' interests and specifically their dependency on the local community for funding and legitimacy. It was hypothesized that these variables would also have weak direct effects and strong indirect effects on activation. This generally proved to be the case for INFL but not for HDQTLOC.

In the school issue, the curfew issue, the hospital issue, and the airport issue, INFL had either a strong negative or weak direct effect on activation. Only for the post office did it have a moderately strong positive direct effect. In contrast, for every issue but the airport issue this variable had a strong positive indirect effect. Perhaps an explanation similar to the one offered for FUNDS is appropriate here. In this community open pursuit of one's economic self-interest may have been tabooed as well. A more tactful way to gain access to decision-making arenas would be, again, to position oneself in interorganizational networks in order to gain access indirectly.

However, the negative effects of INFL may prove to be even more interesting. We were struck by the fact that, in expressive issues especially, organizations seemed to be active on issues that had nothing to do with their economic interests. For example, organizations that were dependent upon extralocal sources for their funds became directly involved in the school and hospital issues. We suggested earlier that when issues are defined in terms of "locals" versus "cosmopolitans," the loyalties of organizations rather than their economic dependencies may be more important to organizational elites. Interestingly enough, our findings suggest that perhaps some of the "rancor" of these issues may have been caused by the unexpected participation of "cosmopolitans" in local community affairs.

Being headquartered locally (HDQTLOC) behaved more erratically. In the curfew issue and the post office issue, HDQTLOC had strong positive direct effects and no indirect effects; in the school issue it had a negative direct effect and a very weak indirect effect; and in the hospital and airport issues it had almost no effect at all. For two issues (the curfew and post office issues), being based in the local community and thus being more integrated into the local culture and norms was a factor in encouraging participation (see Kasarda and Janowitz, 1974). For the other issues this variable was seemingly unimportant. The weak indirect effects are understandable, if we consider that HDQTLOC was only weakly correlated with MONEY, INFOR, and SUPPORT (see Chapter 3).

We also argued that organizational activities would be critical in explaining activation and that the effect would be direct. We argued that it is in the domain of certain organizations to participate in and resolve community conflicts (see Field, 1970). In four out of our five issues PROBLEM had a positive direct effect on activation. Although the effects of this variable were not always that strong, our findings point to the importance of the organizational domain in explaining involvement in community decision-making.

Finally, we examined the effects of centrality on activation. In four out of the five issues studied, centrality in either the money, information, or support networks had a strong positive direct effect on activation. Only on the hypothetical issue did these variables have no effect. We had suggested several hypotheses that stipulated that centrality in selected networks would be related specifically to activation on certain types of decision. Centrality in the support network was expected to be a better predictor of activation on expressive issues and centrality in the money network more important in explaining activation on instrumental issues. We also hypothesized that centrality in the information network would be critical in all issues. Although there were some exceptions, our results generally supported our hypotheses.

We found that centrality in the support network was critical in explaining activation in the school issue and in the hospital issue and that centrality in the money network was important for participating in the hospital issue. These findings are consistent with our hypotheses because the school issue was clearly expressive and the hospital issue was both expressive and instrumental. We also found that centrality in the information network was an important predictor of activation in the school, curfew, and post office issues. It seems that dominance in information systems gives an organization a special advantage which makes it a valuable addition to decision-making coalitions regardless of the issue. However, we did not find that centrality in the money network predicted activation in the post office issue or that centrality in the support network accounted for activation in the curfew issue. We had expected to find these two relationships in our data.

Discussion

At this point we would like to speculate on the implications of our research for the general study of community structure and decision-making. In light of our findings on organizational activation on community issues, we have further evidence that interorganizational networks of money, information, and support are important social structures in the community. For most of our analyses, it was organizations' positions in these networks and not their individual characteristics that explained their participation in decision-making action sets.

If we can trust our findings, then perhaps we can add a new wrinkle to the debate between the pluralists and the elitists. To review these two positions briefly, pluralists have argued that as one looks at different community issues, one finds different actors in different areas of community life being activated (e.g., Dahl, 1961; Rose, 1967). On the other hand, the elitists have argued that even though this may be true, it seems that economic actors are always benefiting most in community decisions (e.g., Hunter, 1953).

Our findings suggest that perhaps both theories are correct. We found that positions in different community structures were important in explaining the activation of organizations on different issues. This supports the pluralist position. As different issues arose affecting different areas of community life, organizations which dominated different institutional structures became active. However, the organizations which dominated these institutions were disproportionately wealthier than other organizations in the community and had a greater economic interest in the community. This may be taken as support for the elitist position. Participation of an organization in community affairs was a function of its structural position in certain institutionalized network structures, but access to the positions seemed to be governed by a competitive process whereby the more resourceful economic interests attained dominant positions.

We suspect that most of the confusion in the literature can be traced to the failure of researchers to recognize that there are two different levels of social action relevant here. Traditionally research has focused either on adaptive processes within the community as the community strives to solve its collective problems (e.g., Turk, 1973a, 1977; Clark, 1968; Aiken and Alford, 1970; Lincoln, 1976) or on the fate of formal organizations within the community as they compete with other formal organizations for scarce resources (e.g., Levine, White, and Paul, 1963; Zald, 1967). In the first case, the community is the unit of analysis, and the focus is on its functional integration. In the second case, organizations within the community are the units of analysis, and the focus is on the competition and stratification of these actors. The integration of the community is never linked to the competitive processes that go on between units within it, and the stratification of organizations is seldom related to the collective problem-solving efforts that the community must undertake.

We think that our research helps to bridge this gap. We have demonstrated that the structural properties of the community as a macrophenomenon (e.g., structural patterns within community institutions) are the by-products of competition among formal organizations on the microlevel. Community structures do exist as social entities in and of themselves. Our finding that interorganizational network structures independently explained organizations' activation in community issues is proof of this. At the same time, however, these structures are the product of intense interorganizational competition and thus will reflect, at least indirectly, the interests of the more resourceful actors in the community. Obviously, taking only a "snapshot" of the community, as we did, does not allow us to appreciate the subtle interplay between the problem-solving efforts of community institutions and the competition among organizations within these institutions. Hopefully, our efforts in this chapter have stimulated enough curiosity concerning these issues, and such analyses will be done in the near future using the more appropriate longitudinal research design.

NOTES

1. In many ways our point of view is similar to that of Van de Ven et al. (1975). The interorganizational structures relevant to different functional needs of the community must be able to react to their environments just as different organizational subsystems must be responsive to their task environments.

2. We should keep in mind that the "delivery systems" which we are referring to are not reifications but rather concrete relational systems (see Turk, 1973a). Demands are made by groups of people, and representatives of organizations which occupy certain positions in concrete network structures make decisions regarding these demands. From our perspective, the success of the "system" in meeting these demands is not contingent upon some ecological fit between organizational forms and environmental conditions (e.g., Hannan and Freeman, 1977); rather its success is dependent upon the current market demands of different constituencies and the foresight and planning of organizational elites in the different network structures.

3. This is not to argue that the lack of controversy necessarily implies that "consumers" are satisfied with the goods and services provided by existing delivery systems. For example, the lack of controversy may be due to the tight control that certain elites exercise over institutional structures. Hunter (1953) and Banfield (1961) documented how economic, managerial, and political elites go to great lengths to insure that controversy is mitigated and that confrontations between organizational power centers and/or population subgroups are avoided. To the extent that formal grievance procedures can be manipulated (Barsky, 1974; Suttles, 1972) and political decisions redefined to satisfy different interest groups, elites can effectively forestall controversy and control the agenda of the community "calendar." This is regardless of how poorly needs are being met in the community.

4. For a critique and defense of the issue approach, see Aiken and Mott (1970: Part IV).

5. The informants included the city planner, the assistant city manager, the president of the real estate board, the executive secretary of the chamber of commerce, the president of a ministers' association, the principal of the community high school, the president of the League of Women Voters, and the local newspaper publisher.

6. The community elite included 77 prominent individuals in Towertown. These individuals were the subjects of Laumann's study of community elites (see Chapter 2). These individuals were chosen on the basis of their positions in community institutions as well as their reputation as community leaders. For a more detailed discussion of how these actors were chosen, see Laumann, Marsden, and Galaskiewicz (1977).

7. Below we have summarized the number of organizations which were reported to be active on an issue by the elite and those whose agents confirmed that they were indeed active.

	School	Curfew	Hospital	Post Office	Airport
Reputed activation	9	10	32	11	10
Self-reported activation	1	5	22	5	9

We are not sure why organizational representatives were so unwilling to say that they participated in a given issue. All we know is that respondents were always willing to discuss the policies and practices of other organizations but not always their own business.

8. These accounts were compiled from interviews with the principal agents of the organizations and other informed community residents. The editing of these accounts was done by Peter Marsden, James Lynch, and the author.

9. The reader should remember that the dependent variable for each analysis is a dummy variable for organizational activation and that the distribution for each variable is highly skewed (see Table 4.2). Our results, then, should be interpreted cautiously.

10. The signs for correlations and regression coefficients involving the centrality scores have all been reversed as they were in Chapter 3.

Chapter 5

COMMUNITY RESOURCE NETWORKS
AND POLITICAL INFLUENCE

So far we have described the positioning of organizations within three resource networks in Towertown. We have also identified the participants in different community issues and described the positions that they occupied in these networks. In this chapter we are more concerned with explaining just how organizations' positions in these networks affect their overall influence in community affairs and their chances of winning and losing in specific community decision-making situations. We suspect that an organization's success in community decision-making is a function of the direct linkages which it has with other actors in the respective networks of money, information, and support as well as the resources which it controls.

Resources, Resource Mobilization, and Community Power

In most any decision-making situation there will be different opinions on the way that a particular problem should be solved.

The simple fact that actors become involved in a particular issue, either because of their interest in the problem or because others in the community expect them to be responsible for the maintenance of certain institutional sectors of the community, does not mean that they will all be of one mind in addressing the problem. As we suggested in Chapter 4, an action set emerges in response to certain demands in the environment; yet parties in the action set may very well have different points of view. In this chapter we will analyze the relative success and failure of the organizations which became involved in each of the five issues as well as the overall influence in community affairs of all organizations in the community.

Several factors might explain why some actors are more influential than others. Both pluralists and elitists have commented extensively on the relationship between resources and political influence (see French and Raven, 1959; Dahl, 1961; Gamson, 1966b; Clark, 1968; Coleman, 1971; and Laumann and Pappi, 1976). Both schools agree that the actor or actors who control highly valued resources are more likely to "get what they want" in the community. The difference between the two perspectives is in their description of how resources are distributed among actors in the American community. The pluralists see resources as widely dispersed throughout the system; the elitists argue that resources are more concentrated. However, there seems to be little disagreement that resources are important for the exercise of power.

An actor's influence, however, usually does not rest solely on his own resources. Often an actor must be able to mobilize the resources of other actors as well. This is typically done through coalition formation. Two general types of coalitions are found in the literature: the *issue specific coalition* which comes out of the pluralist tradition and the *institutional coalition* which comes out of the elitist tradition.

Issue specific coalitions are formed by independent actors who rationally decide to "deal" some of their resources for support on a particular issue. They may pool resources with other actors to get a single measure passed, or they may engage in logrolling where they promise future support to other actors in return for support on a decision which they have a greater interest in. Whether the coalition is for one issue or across a series of issues, actors are expected to act in their own self-interest at all times and to construct their coalitions through a bargaining process.[1]

Institutional coalitions are much different. Rather than being loosely structured, special purpose social arrangements which actors freely negotiate among themselves in the face of different decisions, these coalitions are usually permanent community fixtures. This type of coalition is made up of actors who are dependent upon one another for a wide range of goods and services and thus are obligated to support one another's position on issues (e.g., Hunter, 1953). These dependency relations are often quite complex, covert, and hierarchially structured. At times they take on the character of "conspiracies." In the spirit of Bachrach and Baratz (1962, 1963), we would argue that the coalitions which develop around specific issues (or across a series of issues) are almost totally irrelevant, for the networks among certain actors are often so tightly structured that they can even determine the sorts of issues that emerge in the first place. The distribution of resources among actors and the ongoing, structural linkages which exist among actors prior to any single issue affect the overall course of community decision-making to a much greater extent than the ad hoc coalitions which develop after an issue has emerged in the public arena. Perrucci and Pilisuk (1970) argue that these networks constitute the community's power structure.

Although these two models purport to explain who "wins" and "loses" in community decision-making, we are still skeptical. On the one hand, the pluralist position seems incredibly naive, for it virtually ignores the presence of informal, institutionalized, dependency relations among actors in the community (see Marsden and Laumann, 1977). On the other hand, the elitist position is almost paranoid; systems are just too complex for tightly integrated, omnipotent conspiracies to prevail. Consequently, an alternative model is needed which can explain more realistically how coalitions are used to mobilize resources and, in turn, explain the power of actors in a community political system. We think that a model which is more sensitive to actors' position in institutional resource networks will help to remedy the situation, drawing on the strengths of both perspectives while avoiding their weaknesses.

A Latent Structural Model of Community Decision-Making Processes

A quick survey of the literature indicates that issues seldom develop to the point where all interested actors are brought into a controversy and all available resources are mobilized (see Banfield, 1961; Dahl, 1961; Coleman, 1957). For numerous reasons complete mobilization would be disastrous for almost all parties involved.[2] More often we find that elected officials, bureaucrats, and committees responsible for making certain political decisions take into account the opinions of various groups in the community that do become active, assess these actors' potential to form coalitions with other actors in the community, and then make decisions accordingly so as to minimize the level of conflict over the issue. This process is described narratively in several accounts of decision-making in large metropolitan areas (see Caro, 1974; Hayes, 1972; and Rakove, 1976). Proposals which would threaten potentially powerful interests are regarded by decision-makers simply as "absurd" or "irresponsible" and are thus ignored. The successful politician is one who is sensitive to the potential coalitional partners that different groups may recruit without ever having to actually "test the waters." We would argue that it is in this way that actors are successful in different decision-making situations and not through the actual activation of allies.

Needless to say, this model certainly differs from the pluralist and elitist models. In our model an actor really never mobilizes his own resources or the resources of others. His success is a function of the probability that he could form a coalition with resourceful actors in the community if he wanted to. Decision-makers only peruse the situation and make decisions so as to minimize conflict. Actors neither mobilize other actors' resources by bargaining their way into issue specific coalitions nor do they mobilize others' resources by "calling in their notes" and activating an institutional coalition. Rather, once their opinions are made known, they just wait and see what decision-makers will do (see Banfield, 1961).

Our model differs from the pluralist and elitist models in other ways as well. For example, interested parties are not the ones who decide the issue. All too often pluralists give the erroneous impression that any actor in the private sector can get together with other private sector actors, strike a bargain among themselves and lay their decision before the appropriate governmental officials, who readily rubber-stamp their "deal." Our model rejects this point of view entirely. It also rejects the idea that public decision-makers are the pawns of business or party interests. Our perspective sees public decision-makers as taking an active role in the political process anticipating the needs, wishes, and potential coalitional strength of different actors in the community. Public officials are not simply "window dressing" that elites use to disguise their own control over community institutions.

EVALUATING THE COALITIONAL POTENTIAL OF ACTORS

Although it is relatively easy to assess an actor's resources, it is not all that easy to judge an actor's potential to form political coalitions. We will argue that the probability of an organization mobilizing the resources of other organizations is a function of how proximate it is to other corporate actors in communitity institutions. Laumann and Pappi (1976) found this to be true for organizations in the communities they studied. In Altneustadt coalitions of organizations reflected the proximity of organizations in the networks of overlapping memberships. In effect, the "closer" organizations were to one another, the more likely they were to take the same position on an issue.

Although reduced social distance may increase the probability that two actors will form a coalition, it is not clear just why this should be. Two very different models might explain this phenomenon. The first we will call the *support model*. Here organizations would support other organizations politically because of loyalty. Organizations which interact with one another regularly are likely to develop common interests and to trust one another. If an actor becomes politically involved, those actors which routinely provide goods and services to it will likely support it in times of political crisis as well. There may be some pay-offs in the long run; however, actors are motivated primarily out of loyalty to those which they already support. The second model will be called the *dependency model*. Here actors would come to the aid of other actors because they are obligated to them for some reason or another (see Emerson, 1962; Blau, 1964). Organizations may be dependent upon some actor for goods and services; consequently, when that actor gets politically involved, they may very well give him their political support. Here motives are more selfish. Dependent actors fear that their supplier will cut off their resources if they refuse to support him. In all likelihood, dependent organizations will welcome the opportunity to support more dominant actors because this would help to equalize their relationship.

Whether one model or the other is more appropriate for any given community will probably be affected by the size, composition, and history of the community. In terms of our general argument it makes little difference. The important point is that the growth of elaborate resource exchange systems could put some actors in very strong bargaining positions vis-a-vis authorities. To the extent that actors develop extensive working ties with one another, a power structure of sorts does evolve. Even though these networks linkages may never actually be used to mobilize resources to support a political position, the potential coalitional strength of some actors could be so formidable that political decision-makers would always think twice before challenging these actors' interests.

WHY DOES IT WORK?

This "politics by default" works so well because it benefits a number of actors in the community. On the one hand, it gives authorities and public decision-makers at least the appearance of autonomy and control over the community. Authorities are still perceived by the public as taking the initiative in public matters and providing "leadership." In the eyes of their constituents they are very influential and respected, and this deference is not completely unfounded. Authorities do make decisions autonomously, and they may very well have no ties or obligations to special interests in the community. So long as authorities make the "right" decisions, there is no need on the part of potentially powerful interests to react and create a disturbance. Authorities are simply doing "a good job" and preserving social order.

Even if authorities make the "wrong" decisions, they will probably still escape retribution. Interest groups, though offended, are not likely to engage in conflict strategies hastily. Actors must first carefully weigh the consequences of activating a coalition, for activation would entail transforming their day-to-day contacts into real-life political activists. Such a course of action is very risky. Actors are often unsure if they can convert their business and personal contacts into political allies because these contacts also have "contacts" and obligations to others in the community. Even more importantly, actors are never really sure who their true antagonists are. Authorities are usually the immediate opponents; however, there is often a vague feeling that there are other actors in the community who are in favor of the decision and that they will mount a counteroffensive if anyone challenges the decision. Often this feeling is found among out-groups (e.g., racial and ethnic minorities) where there is a belief that the "system" is out to get them. Although both decision-makers and academics scoff at this paranoia, these groups' anxieties may not be all that unreasonable. If our model is correct, powerful interest groups will "lay back" to see what happens, and they may become active given a disappointing turn of events. If marginal groups become politically active at all, it is perhaps more a testimony to their naivete or despair than to the openness of the political system.

Many actors in the private sector should find the situation advantageous as well. In our model more resourceful and well-connected actors need not expend their resources or activate their contacts to exercise political influence. An actor can "get what he wants" politically simply by pursuing its own day-to-day business.

For example, this is often the situation for large economic actors who can insure their influence in the community simply by establishing overlapping board memberships among themselves. The actual recruitment of board personnel may have little to do with political considerations (Allen, 1974; Pfeffer, 1972; Aldrich and Pfeffer, 1976); however, we suspect that the political impact of board interlocks is far reaching. Extensive board interlocks can effectively intimidate potential adversaries and decision-makers alike. Although the organizations represented on the boards are not political allies per se, they are potential coalition partners.

Another advantage to special interest groups is that if conflict does break out, either because authorities are insensitive to the political realities in their environment or simply are unable to avoid offending one interest or another, the "fallout" will likely remain in the public sector. Because interest groups do not exercise influence directly, authorities alone are held accountable and blamed for their lack of "judgment" or "leadership." Subsequently, the most influential actors in the community will likely come through any community controversy virtually unscathed.

Resource Networks and the Generation of Political Influence

Given our model, how can we apply it to the study of decision-making in Towertown or any other community? In this section we will argue that examination of organizations' positions within the resource networks of money, information, and support may be of great use to us.

Traditionally, network analysis has been more useful for describing social structures (see Leinhardt, 1977). This is how we have used network analysis in this study so far. There is, however, another tradition in the social sciences which takes a more process-oriented approach toward social networks. Social networks have been used to help explain the spread of innovations (e.g., Coleman, Katz, and Menzel, 1966; Aldrich, 1976), the integration of a job market (e.g., Granovetter, 1974), political mobilization (e.g., Perrucci and Pilisuk, 1970; Turk, 1973a; Marsden and Laumann, 1977), and economic stabilization (e.g., Allen, 1974; Pfeffer, 1972; Zald, 1967). In each of these contexts, networks have been interpreted as avenues through which information or resources flow so as to bring about greater coordination or integration among a set of actors in a group or social organization. The various social processes alluded to above are facilitated or retarded by the network ties that exist among actors.

Our intention in this section is to demonstrate how networks are important in transforming economic resources in a community into political resources. The crux of our argument above was that an actor's day-to-day transactions with other actors in his environment constitute a set of bonds which can be utilized to further the actor's political interests. That is, an actor's network ties are the avenues through which other actors' resources can be transformed into political influence for that actor. We will call these resources an actor's "interorganizational resources." Since we argued that public decision-makers decide issues on the basis of each actor's potential capacity to create political coalitions, an actor's day-to-day contacts in the community become all important in determining just what this potential is.

One way to think about this is to argue that an organization's influence in community affairs is a function of his contacts via money, information, and support multiplied by the monetary resources of these contacts. In other words, one could estimate an actor's potential coalitional strength by merely summing up the resources of those actors which he has routinized, continuous relations with. If one believes that the most important interorganizational contacts are an actor's "support" linkages, then one needs to sum across those actors who give money, information, and moral support to him. If one believes that the most important interorganizational contacts are an actor's "dependency" linkages, then one needs to sum across those who receive money, information, and moral support from the actor. Algebraically, for a given population of actors and a given network of resources the relationship between resources, influence, and network inflows can be expressed as follows:

$$A_{n \times n} (R_n) = P_n$$

and the relationship between resources, influence, and network outflows:

$$\overline{A}_{n \times n} (R_n) = P_n$$

where A is the asymmetric n x n adjacency matrix of a given type of linkage, R is the vector of resources for all actors n in the population, and P is the vector of influence scores for all actors n.

Algebraically, we could argue that the matrix representation of the digraph describing the network that exists among a set of actors is equivalent to the coordinates of a matrix representation of some linear transformation of the original re-source vector. To think of this matrix/vector product in this way is theoretically very appealing. One can easily conceive of some function (e.g., a set of social relationships) as transforming a vector in one social space (e.g., a set of economic resources—money) into a vector in another social space (e.g., a set of political resources—influence). Phrasing this a little differently, we can think of a set of social relations as the effective means by which resources in one area of community life (e.g., the economy) are transformed into resources useful in another (e.g., the polity). In this way we can talk about how resources in a social system are mobilized for power.[3] Needless to say, the manner in which resources are mobilized or transformed will differ considerably across communities depending upon the patterns within relational systems. Also it will differ if one focuses on inflow or outflow vectors. Our argument simply states that if we are going to determine the capacity of a social organization to translate re-sources into collective action, then we must pay attention to the existing set of relationships among community actors as well.

Hypotheses

H14: The greater the amount of money controlled and the greater the number of people affiliated with an organization, the more others in the community will view it as influential in community affairs.

H15: The greater the amount of money controlled and the greater the number of people affiliated with an organization, the more success-ful it will be in different community decision-making situations.

H16: Organizations which are involved in community problem solving will be perceived by other actors to be very influential in community affairs.

H17: Organizations which are involved in community problem solving will be more successful in different community decision-making situations.

As we argued above, the resources of an actor are going to contribute to its overall influence in community affairs and to its success in different issues. Organizations that control resources which others value (e.g., money and "people") are going to get their way in community affairs more often than not. As decision-makers evaluate the political arena, they obviously are going to respect organizations which control resources that can be used against them.

The importance of organizational activities/function is based on a somewhat different argument. In our model, decision-making bodies are autonomous actors in the community who reserve the right to pursue one public policy or another as they see fit. That they are sensitive to the political realities enhances rather than detracts from their influence. As long as these actors make decisions which do not offend powerful interest groups, they should be very influential in community affairs and successful in various issues.

H18: The greater the amount of money that an organization's interorganizational contacts control, the more others in the community will view it as influential in community affairs.

H19: The greater the amount of money that an organization's interorganizational contacts control, the more successful it will be in different community decision-making situations.

These hypotheses simply summarize our arguments in the section above. The resources of organizations with which an actor has routine contact should greatly affect how other actors perceive him. If an actor's interorganizational partners have a great deal of money, then the actor will be viewed as potentially very influential in the community because he has the potential to mobilize very powerful coalitions. This view of the organization will be reflected in other actors perceiving him as very influential in community affairs and decision-makers pursuing policies which are in line with his positions on various issues.

Either mode of resource conversion may be effective in our case community. Therefore, we will test both the "support" and "dependency" models with our data. Because of the small size of the community and its homogenity, we suspect that organizations with more resourceful support linkages will tend to be more influential and successful than organizations with more resourceful dependency linkages. Because of the *gemeinschaft* quality of social relations in a community of this sort, the coalitional potential of actors will likely depend more upon the loyalty of their current supporters than upon the fears and anxieties of those who they support.

Methodology

Our hypotheses test not only the effects of organizations' resources and activities on their influence in community affairs but also the effects of actors' interorganizational resources. Organizations' resources and activities are measured the same way that they were before. The resource variables include the amount of funds (FUNDS) and people (PERS) organizations control; for activities we again used a dummy variable identifying problem-solving organizations (PROBLEM). All of these variables will be included both in a multiple regression analysis of the reputed and actual influence of organizations and in an analysis of winners and losers in four community issues. As these variables were described earlier (see Chapter 3), we need not discuss them any further here.

Our measures of actors' interorganizational resources are much different from any of the other empirical indicators we have used thus far. However, the actual computation of these matrix/vector products is relatively straightforward. As we are interested in both inflows and outflows of money, information, and moral support, we use the three asymmetric matrices for these resources in our analysis. The diagonals remain set to zero, because at this point we are not interested in measuring the effects of an organization's own resources on its influence and success. To ascertain the amount of interorganizational resources that can be recruited from an actor's current *support system,* each matrix is simply multiplied by a vector containing the amounts of money each organization controls.[4] The products are three vectors which contain the amounts of money each actor could tap if the organizations which currently provide it with money, information, and support would become politically active on its behalf (MONEY-FUNDS, INFOR-FUNDS, SUPPORT-FUNDS). For example, the first entry in the MONEY-FUNDS vector is the amount of money that the Farm

Association could tap if all the actors who give it money would give it access to all the money they control. The first entry in the INFOR-FUNDS vector is the amount of money the Farm Association could tap if all the actors who give it information would give it access to all the money they control. To arrive at the interorganizational resources to be recruited from an actor's current *dependency relations*, the transpose of each matrix is multiplied by the vector of money resources. The products of these functions are three vectors which contain the amounts of money each actor could tap if the organizations to which he currently is giving money, information, and moral support decided to back his political interests.

Once these variables were computed, we recoded them to give them a more normal distribution. We then correlated them with measures of organizations' relative influence in community affairs. To get an "influence" score for each actor we asked our respondents to specify which organizations they felt were especially influential in community affairs (see Aiken and Mott, 1970). Respondents could name as many organizations as they wished. An influence score for each actor was then tabulated simply by counting the total number of times that it was mentioned as being "very influential" by our respondents (INFLUENCE).

We also want to know how well actors did across the four "real" issues we described earlier. Eventually, we will also describe the characteristics of these actors who "won" and "lost" on the issues. The positions of organizations were taken from the questions we asked our elite respondents on the participation of organizations in different issues.[5] Organizations that received more nominations as being for a proposal than against it were scored as being in favor of it; those that had more nominations as being against a proposal than for it were scored as being opposed to it. Actors that either did not take a position or had an equal number of nominations as being for or against a proposal were considered to be neutral.

In the community there was general consensus as to which sides won and lost on the different issues. On the school issue, the actors that wanted to close the Garvey School won. Actors that were in favor of the illegal curfew won on that issue. The proponents of the new health services center finally got their facility built. Finally, the new post office on the east end of the central business district was built despite the protests of those who wanted it on the west end of town. In Table 5.1 we present the number of actors in our population who were "winners," "losers," and "neutrals" on each issue.

Although we will analyze each issue separately we also want to arrive at an overall indicator of an actor's success. The strategy we chose was to compute a type of "batting average" for each actor which would also be sensitive to the number of times that he "went to bat" in the political arena. Indeed, an actor that lost every issue (0 for 4) was less successful than an actor that lost on the only issue that he got involved in (0 for 1). Similarly, an actor that went "four for four" was more successful than one that went "one for one." To take these considerations into account, a nine

Table 5.1: Frequency Distribution of Organizations' Reputed Positions on Four Community Issues

	Winners	Nonparticipants	Losers
School issue	1	64	8
Curfew issue	7	64	2
Hospital issue	28	43	2
Post office issue	4	62	7

Table 5.2: Scheme for Coding Organizations' Success in Four Community Decisions and Frequency Distribution

Wins/Total Number of Positions on Issues				Values	Frequency
4/4				4	0
	3/3			3	0
3/4		2/2		2	2
	2/3		1/1	1	21
2/4		1/2		0	10
	1/3		0/1	−1	4
1/4		0/2		−2	0
	0/3			−3	0
0/4				−4	0
0/0				Blank	36
					73

point scale was devised that tried to equivocate actors' records on the issues. Table 5.2 presents both the scale we devised and the frequency distribution for this variable (SUCCESS). We might add that the thirty-six actors that took no position on any issue or that were neutral on all issues were not included in subsequent analyses of SUCCESS.

Analysis

Our analysis will be presented in two parts. First, we will analyze the reputed influence of organizations (INFLUENCE) and organizations' overall success rate (SUCCESS). We will examine zero-order correlations and perform regression analyses to determine the relative effects of the different organizational and interorganizational variables on INFLUENCE and SUCCESS. Special attention will be given to the effects of MONEY-FUNDS, INFOR-FUNDS, and SUPPORT-FUNDS. The second part of the analysis will identify just who was successful on each of the four issues. We will describe "winners," "losers," and "neutrals" by examining the mean values of each of our different variables for each category of actors.

GENERAL COMMUNITY INFLUENCE

Table 5.3 presents the zero order correlations between the organizational variables, the interorganizational resource variables, and our measures of organizational influence.[6] To begin with, we see that INFLUENCE and SUCCESS are weakly correlated. That is, there is no significant relationship between an actor's reputed influence and his actual successes and failures. There has been debate in the decision-making literature for years over the advantages and disadvantages of various measures of influence (Aiken and Mott, 1970). Our findings suggest that each indicator is measuring something quite different and call into question the argument that an actor's reputation is simply based on his "track record."

Looking at the correlations of the six interorganizational resource variables with INFLUENCE, we find strong positive asso-

Table 5.3: Correlation Matrix, Means, Ranges, and Standard Deviations for Selected Organizational Variables, Interorganizational Resource Variables, and Measures of Organizational Influence

	INFLUENCE	SUCCESS	FUNDS	PERS	PROBLEM	Mean	S.D.	Range	N
Organizational influence									
INFLUENCE	1.000					24.48	18.53	2–67	73
SUCCESS	.081	1.000				.56	.76	-1–2	37
Organizational resources									
FUNDS	.322	.277	1.000			4.19	2.41	1–8	73
PERS	.143	-.099	.255	1.000		4.60	2.46	1–8	73
Organizational activities									
PROBLEM	.263	-.056	-.527	-.145	1.000	.52	.50	0–1	73
Interorganizational resources (inflows only)									
MONEY-FUNDS	.411	.087	.343	-.141	-.118	3.57	1.12	1–6	73
INFOR-FUNDS	.433	-.123	.271	-.013	-.029	3.53	1.20	1–6	73
SUPPORT-FUNDS	.332	.041	.370	-.017	-.144	3.53	1.20	1–6	73
Interorganizational resources (outflows only)									
MONEY-FUNDS	.533	.048	.513	.256	-.089	3.54	1.17	1–6	73
INFOR-FUNDS	.506	.012	.290	-.134	-.052	3.53	1.20	1–6	73
SUPPORT-FUNDS	.547	.024	.326	.075	.016	3.53	1.20	1–6	73

ciations. Organizations which are perceived as being very influential in the community have interorganizational linkages (both inflows and outflows) to very wealthy actors. A skeptic might argue that more extensive network contacts increase the visibility of an organization and thus artificially increase its reputation as being very influential. In response, one might say that these networks are important community structures, and that it is position in these structures which make actors' influential. Regardless of the interpretation, there is clearly a strong association between interorganizational resources and organizations' reputed influence. The zero-order correlations between the six interorganizational resources and actors' success rates (SUCCESS) are not that impressive. From these results, the resources of actors' interorganizational contacts do not seem to affect actors' chances of winning and losing in actual decision-making situations.

The simple correlations between our influence variables and organizational resource and activities variables follow a somewhat different pattern. The correlations of SUCCESS and INFLUENCE with FUNDS are high while the correlations with PERS are low. Problem-solving organizations have a slight tendency to be viewed as more influential in community affairs, but to its success an organization's activities are unrelated in community issues.

Finally, the correlations between the interorganizational resource variables and FUNDS are high while the correlations of these network variables with PERS and PROBLEM are low. Not surprisingly, organizations with more economic resources tend to have interorganizational linkages to other wealthy actors.

Table 5.4 presents four step-wise regression models.[7] The first two test the effects of actors' inflow and outflow linkages on their reputed influence; the second two test the effects of inflow and outflow linkages on their success rate. In these models FUNDS, PER, and PROBLEM are entered first, and the respective sets of interorganizational resource variables are entered in turn.[8] The object of this analysis is to see how much of the variance in INFLUENCE and SUCCESS can be explained by entering sets of interorganizational resource variables. Also, we hope to compare the relative effects of all the variables in the model on our dependent variables.

Table 5.4: Regression Analysis for Organizations, Reputed Influence (INFLUENCE) and Success on Four Community Issues (SUCCESS)

	N = 68	INFLUENCE		N = 35	SUCCESS	
		Inflow Variable Effects	Outflow Variable Effects		Inflow Variable Effects	Outflow Variable Effects
Organizational resources						
FUNDS	.594	.398	.276	.468	.551	.663
PERS	.074	.143	.099	−.398	−.514	−.367
Organizational activities						
PROBLEM	.552	.520	.446	.051	−.006	.074
Interorganizational resources						
MONEY-FUNDS	—	.155	.212	—	−.376	−.343
INFOR-FUNDS	—	.238	.301	—	−.047	−.064
SUPPORT-FUNDS	—	.114	.183	—	.196	.090
R^2	.327	.454	.557	.202	.305	.277

We see that the addition of the interorganizational outflow variables is more important in explaining INFLUENCE than the introduction of the interorganizational inflow variables. We should note, however, that both significantly increase the R^2 for INFLUENCE. Substantively, these are important findings. They indicate that the resources of the actors that are dependent upon an organization for money, information, and support affect the reputed influence of that organization more than the resources of the actors that give that organization money, information, and support. Our respondents seem to believe that organizations on which a number of wealthy actors depend are more influential in community affairs. We might add that the effect of funds is much less after each set of interorganizational variables is added.[9] This suggests that having linkages to actors with money, rather than simply having money, may be an important resource, which observers have overlooked. This, of course, would explain why organizations, such as banks and savings and loan associations, are typically respected in a community.

One variable, however, proves resistant to the effects of our interorganizational resource variables. This is the dummy variable designating whether an organization was a community problem solver (PROBLEM). The strong effect of PROBLEM is evidence that certain organizations, simply because of their role as community decision-making organizations, are regarded as being more influential. This strengthens Field's (1970) argument that a division of labor exists among community actors. It also strengthens Levine and White's (1961) argument that organizational domains are operative in community interorganizational fields.

The addition of the interorganizational resource variables has a much different effect on the model explaining SUCCESS. With the addition of interorganizational inflow variables, R^2 increases from .202 to .305; however, the effects of FUNDS and PERS become stronger, and the effect of MONEY-FUNDS is negative. The only anticipated effect is that SUPPORT-FUNDS is positively associated with SUCCESS. The "winners" here are then wealthier and smaller organizations which receive moral support from other wealthy organizations. This, of course, is in contrast to the profile of actors who are perceived as being very influential.

When the interorganizational outflow variables are added, the effect of FUNDS once again becomes stronger; however, the effect of PERS stays about the same. The only interorganizational variable that has any effect is MONEY-FUNDS, but this effect is unexpectedly negative.

WINNING AND LOSING ON FOUR COMMUNITY ISSUES

Analyzing the differences among winners, losers, and neutrals on individual issues is more complicated than analyzing actors' reputed influence in community affairs or their overall success rate. In Table 5.5 we present the mean values of selected organizational and interorganizational resource variables for the three types of actors.[10] In our discussion we will try to assess the relative impact of each variable by contrasting the characteristics of those who won with those who lost.[11]

Table 5.5: Average Values of Selected Organizational and Interorganizational Variables for "Winners," "Losers," and "Neutrals" on Four Community Issues

	SCHOOL ISSUE *expressive*			CURFEW ISSUE *expressive*			HOSPITAL ISSUE *mixed*			POST OFFICE ISSUE *instrumental*		
	Winners	Neutrals	Losers	Winners	Neutrals	Losers	Winners	Neutrals	Losers	Winners	Neutrals	Losers
Organizational resources												
FUNDS*	5.40	1.22	3.76	1.83	1.58	2.40	3.05	.39	5.01	2.51	1.02	5.56
PERS.	680.00	403.14	601.25	122.28	476.25	14.00	433.21	443.70	61.00	33.25	445.74	509.28
Organizational activities												
PROB	1.00	.47	.87	.85	.48	.50	.46	.53	1.00	.75	.52	.43
Interorganizational resources (inflows)												
MON-FUNDS*	15.04	16.19	14.31	16.02	16.12	11.15	22.17	12.38	6.33	8.64	13.18	44.90
INFOR-FUNDS*	57.02	36.02	39.13	64.54	32.16	82.76	43.21	31.46	56.25	49.77	33.25	59.23
SUPPORT-FUNDS*	52.21	21.98	29.07	29.70	23.03	4.55	29.95	19.07	16.26	20.80	21.99	34.98

*The figures for FUNDS, MON-FUNDS, INFOR-FUNDS, and SUPPORT-FUNDS are in the millions.

As expected, in the two more espressive issues the winners tended to control more resources than the losers. In the school issue, the activists who favored closing the Garvey school controlled, on the average, more money and more "bodies" than those who opposed the closing of the school. In the curfew issue, we find a slightly different pattern. Those that were in favor of the curfew had more people available than those who opposed it. We also see that in both issues, community decision-making organizations favored the outcomes.

Also, as we had hypothesized, the interorganizational contacts of the actors that were winners had more money than the interorganizational contacts of those who lost. Since resource inflows were more important than outflows in explaining SUCCESS, we present only the average funds of organizations' "supporters." Linkages via moral support seemed to be especially important for winners. In both cases the supporters of the winners tended to have considerably more money than supporters of the losers. On the other hand, linkages via money and information exchanges do not seem to be that effective in influencing the decision-making process. While the winners of the school issue had access, via information contacts, to more money than the losers, the winners of the curfew issue had access, via information contacts, to less funds than losers. Looking at the available interorganizational resources via money linkages, there is no appreciable difference between winners and losers on either issue.

Our hypotheses are not so clearly supported in the cases of the two more instrumental issues. To begin with, neither resources nor the activities of organizations had a consistently positive effect on either issue. In both cases, poorer rather than wealthier organizations got their way, and only on the hospital issue did larger organizations prevail over smaller ones. Similarly, the activities of organizations did not have a consistent effect. While the winners of the post office issue tended to be problem-solving organizations, the winners of the hospital issue were not.

Looking at the interorganizational resources of actors, we again find only scant support for our hypotheses. In fact, only on the hospital issue did the resources of organizations' supporters seem to make a difference. Actors that gave winners moral support and

money tended to be wealthier than the moral and financial supporters of the losers. However, on the post office issue it is clear in
every instance that the losers had access to more interorganizational money than the winners. That losers tended to have more
money and access to more interorganizational money than winners
obviously goes against our hypotheses. It also is in contrast to our
findings for the two more expressive issues.

When we try to figure out just why different actors won and
lost on these two issues, it seems that very few things counted. In
a way, our hypotheses are strengthened considering that the only
thing which might have enabled the proponents of the hospital to
get their project through was that they had routinized money and
support flows from some of the wealthiest actors in the community. Going back to our journalistic description of the issue, this
seems like a plausible explanation. Throughout its history, the
project was the pet of the business community and thus a strong
impact of MONEY-FUNDS and SUPPORT-FUNDS on the issue's
resolution would not be surprising.

The explanation of who won and lost in the case of the post
office is more straightforward, and again in a way supports our
hypotheses. It is clear that the only reason the proponents of the
east end location won is that they tended to be local community
decision-makers. Rather than reacting to the different interest
groups that became active on the issue as we expected, decision-
makers took the initiative. From our fieldnotes we learned that city
officials were directly drawn into this issue because of their
responsibility for administering federal dollars. The fact that proponents had only the authority of their role as an advantage over
the opposition gives evidence that certain problem-solving roles are
operative in community decision-making systems. Furthermore, it
suggests that these culturally defined "positions" have a certain
clout independently of the organizational and interorganizational
resources of the actors that occupy them.

Discussion

It is clear that systems of community influence are quite complex. An actor's influence, whether it be measured in terms of

reputation or success in community decisions, cannot be predicted simply on the basis of his own resources and activities. Organizations' funds and functional role in the community were important in almost all our analyses. Only in the hospital issue were they unimportant. However, we found that the resources of actors' interorganizational contacts might also be critical in explaining the influence of organizations. More specifically, actors on whom wealthier organizations depended for money, information, and support tended to be seen as more influential in community affairs while organizations that had the moral support of wealthier actors tended to be more successful in various issues. Particularly in the more expressive issues, linkages of moral support may have been very important in mobilizing the resources of other actors.

These findings certainly are not conclusive, but they do provide some support for our theory. The strength of the interorganizational resource variables in our analyses suggests that decision-makers and other actors in the community respect the potential of well-connected actors to establish powerful political coalitions. The fact that the resources of an actor's outflow and inflow partners might be transformed into a reputation for being influential and successful on issues was evidence of this. Needless to say, our analysis is quite rudimentary, and more sophisticated modeling is certainly needed to draw out the more subtle complexities of resource transformative processes.

Some implications of these findings, however, are quite interesting. Returning to a point raised in Chapter 1, we see that the stratification of actors in a community setting cannot be determined simply by inspecting the distribution of resources among individual actors. The resources that one controls certainly contribute to one's influence, but the researcher must also take into account the set of resources that actors can mobilize through their existing set of social relationships. This seems critical even though these network ties may appear to have little to do with political action. Needless to say, our analysis of organizations can be extended to an analysis of individuals and population subgroups. Although this demands a more thorough documentation of all three types of resource networks, the reward of such an effort seems well worth it.

NOTES

1. Political scientists have been in the forefront of analyzing these types of coalitions (see, e.g., Niemi and Weisberg, 1972; deSwann, 1973; Riker, 1962). Sophisticated mathematical models of coalition formation have been constructed which take into account not only the types and amounts of resources which actors control but also actors' rankings of goals, their alternative sources of goal satisfaction, and the constraints which decision rules impose upon them.

2. For an interesting treatment of this phenomenon from the point of view of purposive action theory, see Gamson's (1961) discussion of minimum winning coalitions.

3. We would agree that the analogy between a linear transformation and a social process, such as resource mobilization, should not be overdrawn. However, there is an unusually comfortable fit between what we have always said a set of network linkages can do for actors and the operations of transformative functions on vector elements.

4. Rather than using the recoded values for organizational funds, we used the raw dollar figures. In all subsequent analyses of the interorganizational resource variables, the raw numbers are used.

5. Our panel of experts also indicated the positions that organizations took on the issues in which they became activated (see Chapter 4).

6. Once again we have not reported the levels of statistical significance for our analysis because we are still analyzing a population and not a sample of organizations.

7. List-wise deletion was used for each regression analysis. This means that only 68 cases were analyzed for INFLUENCE and 35 for SUCCESS.

8. Interorganizational resource variables were entered according to the amount of variance they could explain in the dependent variable.

9. The Beta weight for FUNDS dropped most when INFOR-FUNDS was added. For both inflows and outflows this interorganizational variable came first into the model, followed by MONEY-FUNDS and SUPPORT-FUNDS.

10. For the sake of simplicity, we used the raw data for FUNDS and PERS as well as for SUPPORT-FUNDS, INFOR-FUNDS and MON-FUNDS.

11. Needless to say, it would have been much more desirable to use multivariate statistical techniques (e.g., discriminant function analysis) to determine the independent effects of the organizational and interorganizational resource variables. The small number of "winners" and "losers" made such an analysis unfeasible.

Chapter 6

SUMMARY, CONCLUSIONS, AND DIRECTIONS FOR THE FUTURE

After reading this short monograph the reader may wonder if, indeed, the author has made "much ado about nothing." We have spent a great deal of time and effort describing interorganizational networks of money, information, and moral support in a small midwestern community. We have also analyzed in detail how decision-makers there went about solving some rather mundane problems. Not only have we looked at just one town, and thus are unable to generalize to a larger population of cities, but the place itself is uninteresting to most readers.

Unlike early case studies in sociology and anthropology, we made no pretense that Towertown is representative of any population of cities; nor do we expect the reader to be enthralled by the intricacies of small town politics. Obviously, these are not the strong points of the monograph. However, although Towertown is certainly not a Chicago nor even a Minneapolis, it is much more complex than the high school classes, monasteries, ocean liners, and street gangs which are usually subjected to structural analysis.

153

Our purpose in undertaking this study was to develop some new and powerful strategies for studying complex social organizations, such as communities and, specifically, the social structures within them. By using structural imagery and network methodologies, we hoped to ground theories of community structure and collective decision-making and to give them clearer empirical meanings.

The Structure of Community Institutions

In developing a set of strategies for analyzing community social structures, we drew on the argument of Mitchell (1969) that the structural components of social institutions could be described by tracing the flows of certain resources among actors within a community. In analyzing interorganizational networks of money, information, and moral support we hoped to describe the structural configuration of actors in community institutions of adaptation, problem-solving, and legitimacy. Once actors' positions in these institutions were recovered, we then tried to explain why actors occupied the positions they did.

First, we wanted to explain why some actors were more central in different institutional structures. From the literature on formal organizations, we identified some of the basic principles which supposedly govern interorganizational behavior. For the most part, organizations are viewed as competitive actors in a market environment. On this premise we generated several hypotheses on which organizations would be more central/dominant in each network. We then subjected these descriptive hypotheses to empirical tests. Our findings showed that organizations which controlled more resources and had an interest in maintaining local institutions tended to be more central in each of the three networks. From our analysis we concluded that a competitive market model probably is most appropriate in explaining the construction of hierarchies in different community institutions.

We also wanted to examine the proximity of actors in different institutions. Although organizations within the community were seemingly in competition with one another, their interaction patterns reflected common concerns about functional problems that each actor had to solve for himself. In our data we found that interaction in the money network tended to be influenced by the auspices of organizations, in the information network by activities, and in the support network by the value commitments of organizational elites.

As we pointed out in Chapter 3, in any social organization the positioning of actors in social institutions will be affected both by the desire of actors to dominate and control their environment as well as by their functional needs. Actors do act selfishly and strive to attain their own goals at the expense of other actors. This must be recognized and incorporated into any analysis of social organizations. Conflict is part of social life. At the same time, we must remember that actors face similar functional problems and will work together to solve these problems. Our hope has been to demonstrate that analyzing institutions as we have enables researchers to describe both forms of participation in the collective life of the community. By approaching these media as social institutions and their flows as social structures, we could describe how actors pursued their self-interests and established pecking orders among themselves, while they contributed to the overall functional integration of the entire community.

The monograph has also demonstrated how positions in the networks affected organizations' fates. Specifically, we have concentrated on how actors' structural positions within the three institutional resource networks affected their participation and influence in community decision-making.

The most important finding in Chapter 4 was that the institutional networks of money, information, and support were important in selecting the actors that would participate in decision-making action sets. By this we mean that certain actors were drawn into different issues because they occupied key positions in different institutional structures. As we noted above, actors which had a greater interest in the community and were more resourceful were more dominant in the three networks. However, it was actors' centrality in the networks, and not their resources or interests, which explained their activation on issues.

Although there are many alternative explanations for these findings, we concluded that being dominant in a social structure, which other actors felt to be functionally important to them, conferred a certain status upon an actor. In turn, this status gave him the capacity as well as the responsibility to engage in community problem-solving. Actors become involved in issues not because their individual interests and resources dictated it nor because they felt compelled out of loyalty to certain collective values. Rather, activation on issues seems to have been a function of organizations fulfilling the role expectations accorded to those who dominated certain institutions. As institutions are threatened, others in the community system will expect dominants to protect their own strategic positions in the institutions as well as remedy any malfunctioning that disrupts the collective life of the community.

Although actors' structural positions in different networks enabled them to participate in different community decisions, not all networks were important in explaining the relative success or failure of actors. After examining several indicators of political influence, we concluded that the resources of organizations that gave moral support to an actor were most critical in explaining that actor's influence in the community. An important part of our argument in Chapter 5 was that for actors to be influential and successful, they need not have resources nor did they have to actually mobilize other actors. Resources would help, but an actor's interorganizational resources would be enough to explain his influence and success in community affairs.

We explained these findings by arguing that actors are influential not because they are cleverer or more capable negotiators in bargaining situations, but because they are embedded in relational systems that allow them to play a "cat and mouse" game with authorities in decision-making situations. As authorities try to decide which course of action would cause the least amount of conflict, they evaluate organizations' networks within existing institutional structures. Eventually, issues are decided one way or another because some actors are seen as being able to raise "more hell" than others if a decision were to go against them.

Our arguments and findings have many implications for future research. First, models of collective decision-making can no longer focus only on actors, events, and resources and ignore the structural linkages which exist among actors (Marsden and Laumann,

1977). As we have seen, these linkages can play a very important part in influencing which actors become activated in community issues. Second, any a priori classification of actors into status positions simply on the basis of their resources should be avoided. The power of an actor in a social organization is based not so much on what he can do with his own resources in a conflict situation, but on the probability that he can get others to use their resources on his behalf. Finally, we might try to understand better the role of shared values in decision-making situations. Going back to Chapter 3, we recall that proximity in the support network was most strongly influenced by shared values. If this is true, then perhaps the mobilization of other actors into a coalition (if it becomes necessary) would be based on appeals to actors' commonly held values and not on some sort of "future payoff," as contemporary decision-making theory would argue. We have no evidence that this was true in our community; however, it is an intriguing proposition that deserves further attention.

Problems and Suggestions

Needless to say, this monograph does not even scratch the surface of what research might be undertaken on the social structure of the urban community. There is still a number of topics that need to be explored, and there is a number of problems in network research that must be solved (see Laumann, Galaskiewicz, and Marsden, 1978). By reviewing some of the shortcomings of our own research, perhaps we can help future researchers to begin to address some of these issues.

STATIC VERSUS PROCESS ANALYSIS

As we pointed out in Chapter 5 most network analyses of social organizations have taken a static approach, simply describing the sets or types of linkages among actors in a sample or a population. Only recently have innovative applications of purposive action models, diffusion models, and stochastic models attempted to interpret network linkages within a process framework. Since the study of network processes is in its infancy, let us review some of the things we ignored but which seem to us to set an agenda for future research.

First, we failed to document the actual negotiation that goes on in the construction of interorganizational networks. We never described how actors bicker, bargain, and finally come up with some sort of "deal" among themselves. For example, we did not even know how much "knowledge" organizational elites had when they engaged in interorganizational transactions. In a small group, individuals are likely to have almost complete information on others' activities so that they can anticipate what the structure of relationships in the group will look like after the bargaining is over. We suspect that the leaders of our organizations had no prior knowledge and probably dealt with one another only with their own set of linkages in mind. Any serious study of network construction must take the knowledge base of actors into account. Perhaps a careful examination of multiple networks is a solution. If the researcher can determine the influence of information transactions on subsequent resource exchanges, he may be able to assess the advantages of having extensive information sources (see Galaskiewicz and Marsden, 1978).

Any study of interorganizational relational processes must also include a detailed analysis of network change. Holland and Leinhardt (1977) and Wasserman (1977) have formulated sophisticated stochastic models that focus on the endogamous factors that could affect how a network changes over time. Their efforts should be encouraged, yet we would hope that researchers would also look at changes in the environment of the network and describe how these affect network change as well. Some researchers have already begun to do this. Allen (1974) and Galaskiewicz and Bulcroft (1978) have documented how corporate interlocking networks have been altered as market conditions and the political environment of business corporations change. Unfortunately, these latter studies focus on only two or three time periods and thus are unable to use many of the more sophisticated modelling procedures available for time series analysis.

SPECIFICATION OF LINKAGES

One of the more apparent flaws in our work is the rather crude measurement of interorganizational linkages. We have already discussed this at some length in Chapter 2. Obviously, there is a number of alternatives to simple binary measures. Marrett (1971) and Van de Ven et al. (1975), for example, list a whole set of relational dimensions that the researcher should pay attention to, e.g., the frequency of contact and the degree of formalization (see also Hall et al., 1977). We wholeheartedly agree with their position and encourage researchers to follow their advice.

It was especially unfortunate that we were unable to record the "amount" of each resource transacted, although there were some advantages to using binary data.[1] As we noted earlier, for money, quantifying ties would have been relatively easy. For the other resources it would have been much more difficult. One suggestion, made elsewhere (Galaskiewicz and Marsden, 1978), would be to have actors rank order their ties to others on the basis of how important each was to them. This might be done by having organizational representatives compare other actors in their community on a single type of linkage. For example, they might indicate how important a particular information source was to them compared to other sources. Alternatively, organizational spokesmen might compare different types of linkages for a single organization. For example, is the money or the information received from a given actor more important? Both sets of comparisons would be helpful in getting a more complete description of the interorganizational relationship. The reader should be cautioned, however, that the mathematical and statistical models for analyzing "weighted" graphs are at a very elementary stage of development (see Harary, Norman, and Cartwright, 1965). As the state of the art now stands, most standard graph analytic techniques and even new methodologies such as blockmodeling and loglinear analysis would find it difficult to analyze matrices with weighted entries.

Another problem which was pointed out to us was that the population of organizations chosen might have a very serious effect on the incidence of certain types of transactions.[2] For example, if we had included retailers in our population, the number and pattern of money flows would probably have been much different. One strategy to overcome bias would be to draw up an exhaustive list of every organization in the community and sample from this list. There are several advantages to this. Both very large and very small organizations would have an equal chance of being studied; there would be no a priori judgment as to which organizations were more important in the community; and organizations could more easily be aggregated into general types and linkages between these types described. In studying larger systems, sampling seems to be absolutely necessary. One problem with this approach, however, is that we would not have the types of simple adjacency matrices that we were able to use in this study. Furthermore, linkages would not be described from the point of view of both actors in a dyad. Part of this problem might be overcome by using some of the techniques developed by Laumann (1973) and Alba and Kessler (1977) for analyzing relational data from sample surveys.

ENVIRONMENTS AND EXTRALOCAL LINKAGES

In analyzing organizational behavior in a community, the researcher must remember that corporate actors must cope with two general types of environments—their local community environment and their respective "functional" environments. For some organizations these environments are more or less the same, e.g., the local public school, the businessmen's association, the local entrepreneur; but for most organizations they constitute two very different arenas of action (see Hall, 1972; Aldrich and Pfeffer, 1976; White, 1974).

In this study we tried to be sensitive to this issue by devising measures of organizational dependency. We rationalized that if organizations received most of their funds from local sources and/or were headquartered locally, then the local community environment would be of more interest to them. Thus they would be more concerned with developments within it. I think that our two measures of organizational dependency were adequate, and they did turn out well in the analyses.

One problem that did plague us was that we assumed that all organizations had the same perception of the community environment regardless of what activities they were involved in. For example, we simply assumed that the racial, ethnic, religious, age, and class composition of the population and the physical layout of the community had the same effect on all organizations whether they were retailers, manufacturers, schools, or whatever. This, of course, is difficult to defend. We can only suggest that future research describe in detail organizations' perceptions of their local community environment and evaluate the extent to which these perceptions influence organizations' behavior.

A more devastating criticism of our research is that we failed to include an analysis of how extralocal environments affected the behavior of organizations in the local community. It might be argued that without an understanding of the threats and uncertainties organizations faced in their regional and national input and output markets, it is impossible to explain their behavior in the local community. Inflation, competition from other organizations, federal and state laws and regulations, and shifting consumer tastes are all extralocal environmental contingencies that may limit the options and shape the behavior of organizations. Studies which have taken an egocentric network approach in studying interorganizational linkages have been fairly successful in controlling for environmental effects. Their solution to this problem has been to choose either organizations which were in the same industry (e.g., Lawrence and Lorsch, 1967) or which engaged in the delivery of the same sort of services (e.g., Aldrich, 1976). Obviously, any study which is more ambitious and looks at a wider range of organizations is not going to have such an easy time of it. The researcher will have to identify conditions in each organization's environment and work out a scheme so that environments can be compared.

ELITES, INTEREST GROUPS, AND FORMAL ORGANIZATIONS

Another issue is how organizations come to define their interests. This was pursued in an earlier piece (Laumann, Galaskiewicz, and Marsden, 1978), but we will review our arguments here briefly. To date, research has been unable to demonstrate how organizational policies are formed with respect to the community. In the earlier paper, we phrased this problem in terms of the "interest generation between persons and organizations" and outlined three perspectives on this topic.

The first is the elitist perspective suggested by the works of Mills (1956), Hunter (1953), and Zeitlin (1974). It views organizations and interorganizational systems as devices through which self-conscious solidarity groups maintain their positions of power. Although it is commonly argued that the "upper classes" or "business elite" are the beneficiaries of interorganizational arrangements, research on political parties in machine cities shows how working class ethnic groups and their leaders also benefit from politically manipulating interorganizational systems (See Rakove, 1976).

The second model, the pluralist model, draws from the writings of Dahl (1961), Bentley (1908), and Truman (1951). Organizations are viewed as interest groups created to protect or enhance the common interests of a group of individuals; interorganizational networks are seen as coalitions of these constituencies. The pluralist model, however, does not assume that organizational leaders constitute a self-conscious elite. Rather, through different mechanisms of control, ultimate authority rests in the members of the organization. The model gives much greater attention to broadly based citizen input into organizational policy.

The final perspective, the organizational model, views the relationship between organizations and persons a little differently than the elitist or pluralist models. Organizations are treated as formally organized corporate groups having certain intrinsic interests. These interests are typically expressed by managers, who act as organizational agents. In this model, individuals have no immutable interests apart from their organizational affiliations, and persons are essentially interchangeable as far as the corporate actor is concerned. This third model has been dominant in the administrative and organizational literatures (e.g., Thompson, 1967; Yuchtman and Seashore, 1967; Levine and White, 1961).

At first glance, it appears to be quite difficult to establish which "interest" governs organizational decision-making in a given community context. In our research we simply assumed that organizational decision-makers were governed by organizational interests rather than class or constituent interests and tested hypotheses based on this assumption.

This is not to say that our research strategies could not be altered so that we could test whether other interests influenced organizational policy. One source of direction is Laumann and Pappi's (1976: Chapter 12) analysis of the interface between members of a community elite and different status groups. By asking a cross-section of the population a series of questions on their linkages to different elite actors, they were able to identify elite-constituency clusters using multidimensional scaling techniques. It seems quite feasible that a similar strategy might be used to establish constituency-organizational linkages and elite-organizational linkages. For example, a sample of community residents might be asked to identify the organizations which they went to for help in personal matters, for aid in lobbying, and for information regarding community affairs. Also, the organizational memberships of the community elite might be readily identified. An organization's "interests" might then be determined by taking an inventory of the attitudes of each organization's constituency and elite members on a series of issues and then comparing them to the actual positions that the corporate actors took when the issues arose in the community. At that point, we would be able to ascertain whether the constituency, elite members, or a unique organizational interest influenced organizational policies the most.

COMPARATIVE STUDIES: A NECESSITY

As we have shown in this chapter, our research has failed to respond to a number of issues related to the study of community interorganizational systems. There is one shortcoming, however, which stands out among all the rest—the lack of comparable data on other interorganizational systems. Without some basis for comparison either across time or with other cities in the same time period, it is impossible to determine causal patterns or to make any definitive theoretical statements about interorganizational behavior.

One way for researchers, such as ourselves, to abdicate their responsibility is to recommend that numerous case studies be undertaken which employ theoretical and research strategies similar to their own. This would set a lengthy agenda for students of the urban community. But it would also be irresponsible on our part. As our methods now exist, this type of research would be virtually impossible in larger systems. In addition, more creative students seldom find it interesting to replicate studies that have already been done.

One alternative strategy, which comes readily to mind, is building on the work of Herman Turk (1973a, 1977). In his comparative analysis of urban interorganizational systems, Turk argued that researchers should focus on the organizational activity of key nodes in interorganizational systems, e.g., the mayor's office, municipal government in general, political parties, citywide voluntary associations, and so on. In an earlier piece Turk's work was criticized (see Laumann, Galaskiewicz, and Marsden, 1978), inasmuch as there was no description of actual interorganizational activity in the communities studied. We do believe, though, that there is merit identifying key nodes in interorganizational systems, but we would favor a subsequent investigation into these organizations' interorganizational linkages to one another and to other actors. The recovery of these egocentric networks could be done very easily, refining the approach that we outlined in this monograph. One might even have respondents for these actors describe the set of linkages among other actors in the communities as well. If this latter strategy is pursued, one must be careful that the position of the respondent in the interorganizational system does not distort his perceptions of linkages among other actors.

Concluding Remarks

The findings of this monograph and the recent work on interorganizational networks (e.g., Levine, 1972; Turk, 1977; Warren, et al., 1974; Perrucci and Pilisuk, 1970; and Laumann and Pappi, 1976) demonstrate beyond a doubt that relational analysis is certainly not limited to the study of small groups. By aggregating individuals into corporate groups, we can study the relationships

between them by describing the relationships between the corporate groups. Although we may occasionally borrow terminology
from the social psychological literature to describe the actors
themselves (e.g., their interests, resources, dependencies, and so
on), the nodes and linkages in interorganizational networks are
certainly phenomena of the macrosocial order (see Turk, 1973a).

Needless to say, the greatest strength of network analysis is that
it enables one to move back and forth from the micro- to macro-
levels. As we stated on the first page of this book, our hope is to
understand better the relationship between the individual actor in
a social organization and the structure of relationships that he
finds himself in. In these chapters we have shown that the characteristics of individual actors influence the configuration of relationships in the larger social organization and that the position of
actors in the larger social structures, in turn, affects the actor's
own subsequent behavior.

Obviously, our research here is only a first step. Because of this,
we have tried in this last chapter to honestly evaluate its strengths
as well as its weaknesses. We have been neither overly modest nor
boastful. As the reader has probably sensed by now, we simply
believe that we have a very powerful set of strategies with which
to study social organizations.

NOTES

1. The main advantage of using simple binary measures of relationships was that we
were able to derive the path distances between actors. This, of course, allowed us to
easily identify the indirect links between actors. Subsequently these path distances were
used as our proximity estimates for the SSA-I.

2. This observation was made by an anonymous reviewer for a paper that the author
did with Peter Marsden (Galaskiewicz and Marsden, 1978).

APPENDIX A: STUDY DESIGN

Our study in Towertown was done in conjunction with a study of community elites by Edward Laumann, Peter Marsden, and the author. In the elite study we replicated a piece of research done in a German community by Laumann and Franz Pappi (1976). The description of the elite population can be found in Laumann, Marsden, and Galaskiewicz (1977) and the methods used to identify the elite in Laumann and Pappi (1976). In Towertown we identified 79 individuals as members of the local elite and interviewed 77. For this monograph these respondents were used as a panel of experts whose responses to a series of questions on community issues helped us to identify the organizations which were active in different issues and the positions of organizational actors on the issues (see Chapters 4 and 5).

As it turned out, many of the respondents from our population of organizational agents were also members of the community elite. Where this was the case, we included the set of questions on interorganizational linkages in the body of the elite questionnaire. At the completion of the elite interviews we had data on 46 out of the 109 organizations on the original organizational list. We then went back and interviewed the agents of 27 more organizations. In Chapter 2 we discuss why we did not interview respondents from all 109 organizations. The questionnaire administered to these 27 agents is presented in Appendix B. All of the items in this questionnaire were included in the elite questionnaire. The interviewing of the elite and nonelite corporate actor agents took place between April, 1974 and September, 1974.

In addition to information on the organizational agents and the linkages between organizations we wanted data on certain characteristics of the organizations and the roles that organizations played in different community issues. As these items were not asked in the initial interview, we conducted follow-up phone interviews with all the organizational agents. The questionnaire for these interviews is in Appendix C. The phone interviews took place in December of 1974.

APPENDIX B: INTERVIEW QUESTIONNAIRE FOR ORGANIZATIONAL AGENTS

Q1. Listed on this card are seven different things which most cities would like to do. (Hand respondent Card B.) However, no one city can do all of these things at the same time. Look through the list please and order them according to their importance, that is, the importance which you allot to each problem in Towertown. Which objective, in your opinion, is most important for Towertown at the present time? Second? Third? Least important?

A) Seeing to it that this city becomes a very attractive place to live—with good residential areas and pleasant, convenient community facilities.

B) Seeing to it that this community has a good climate for business which would encourage economic growth.

C) Seeing to it that the city provides its poor and disadvantaged with a decent life—with adequate food, housing, and opportunity.

D) Seeing to it that this is a city free from harmful strife between economic, religious, or neighborhood groups.

E) Seeing to it that the quality of life here doesn't change much from what it is now; that is, that the size and composition of the population stay about the same.

F) Seeing to it that the city has a government which is efficient, honest, and economical.

G) Seeing to it that the city is a place where citizens play an active role in government.

Q2. We have just said that most communities have to deal with such questions. Depending on how these tasks and problems are solved in

169

different communities, one can identify three different community types. (Hand respondent Card C.)

First, there are those communities in which vigorous conflicts between the same leaders or population groups appear again and again in the handling of community affairs and public measures so that the same persons or groups are always found together in a coalition.

In the second type of community, there is also controversy about various problems, but there are constantly changing coalitions between various groups or persons so that the coalitions are different depending on the problem being considered.

Then there are in the third type, communities in which relatively little argument about public measures takes place because there is a relatively high consensus among the various leaders and groups about what needs to be done.

In general, how would you characterize the situation in Towertown during the past four or five years? Does it fit closer to the first, the second or the third description?

First description
Second description
Third description
Other (Have respondent explain.)

(If the respondent does not accept one of the three types but uses a mixed type, probe.)

Which of the two (three) descriptions still fits closest the relationships in Towertown?

Q3. In your opinion, which of the three situations described would be the ideal situation for your community?

First description
Second description
Third description
Other (Have respondent explain.)

We would now like to discuss briefly five issues that have been important in Towertown during the past four or five years.

Q4. First, we would like to discuss the construction of the new health services center. Have you participated in any way in the decision-making process concerning the center?

Yes (If "yes", ask "Why?")
No

And what was your original position toward the health service center?

For it
Against it

Q5.   Second, there has been much talk recently about the construction of a new municipal airport and who should pay for it. Have you participated in any way in the decision-making process concerning the construction of a new airport?

Yes (If "yes", ask "Why?")
No

Do you think the city or county should absorb the costs for a new airport?

The City
The County

Q6.   Third, let us discuss the curfew that was imposed by the city after the May, 1970 demonstrations. Have you participated in this in any way?

Yes (If "yes", ask "Why?")
No

And what was your original position?

For it
Against it

Q7.   Fourth, one of the key decisions concerning urban renewal of the downtown area was the decision to build a new post office on the east end of Washington highway. Have you participated in the decision-making process concerning the building of a new post office?

Yes (If "yes", ask "Why?")
No

And what was your original position?

For it
Against it

Q8.   Finally, last spring there was much discussion on the relative merits of continuing an alternative education program in the Towertown public schools. Have you participated in the decision-making process concerning this?

Yes (If "yes", ask "Why?")
No

And what was your original position?

For it
Against it

What we have done now is to list a number of individuals who have been active in community affairs during the past few years. Most represent important corporate interests in the Towertown area. Before you answer the following questions be sure that you carefully read over the entire list of names.

Q9. Would you please indicate the three persons from the list with whom you most frequently meet socially (or informally)?

Q10. And when you think of your best friends in Towertown and the surrounding area, would you include the above named persons?

Yes   All three of them?
           Two of them?
           One of them?   Please indicate which ones.
No

Q11. Could you now indicate the three persons on our list with whom you have the closest business or professional contact? (Probe to elicit three names.)

Q12. Could you please indicate the three persons with whom you most frequently discuss community affairs? (Probe to elicit three names.) (If necessary) Could you tell me the three persons with whom you are most likely to discuss problems of Towertown?

Q13. We would also like for you to indicate from our list the persons with whom you most frequently discussed the following issues. (Open-ended)

The construction of the health services center
The construction of a new airport
The imposition of a curfew during the riots
The relocation of the post office

The program in the Towertown school system (Garvey school controversy)

Q14. Here we have tried to put together as complete a list of various groups and organizations to be found in Towertown as we could. (Hand over the group list.) We have numbered the groups and organizations to facilitate talking about them. In your answers, please just give us the group's number. Could you first check those groups which are generally very influential in Towertown? (If doubtful which groups, always let him name the more important groups in his judgment.)

Q15. Can you think of any other influential groups or organizations in Towertown that we may have missed? (Get their specific names and functions if unclear.)

Q16. Which is the most influential group of those you have named?

Q17. Which is in second place?

Q18. And which three groups or organizations would you place in the third position?

Now we would like to ask you some questions about some of the ties that (your organization) has with other organizations in the community. Please remember, that we are interested in the sorts of ties (your organization) has with these other organizations and not in your own personal relations. (Hand over group list.)

Please respond with the number of the organization only. There are no limits on the number of organizations that you might name.

Q19. Which organizations on this list does (your organization) rely upon for information regarding community affairs (or other matters that might affect your organization)?

Q20. And to which organizations on this list would (your organization) be likely to pass on important information concerning community affairs (or other matters that might affect them)?

Q21. Now to which organizations on this list, does (your organization) give (substantial) funds as payment for services rendered or goods received, loans, or donations?

Q22. And from which organizations on this list does (your organization) get (substantial) funds as payments for services rendered or goods provided, loans, or donations?

Q23. Which organizations on this list would (your organization) feel a special duty to stand behind in time of trouble: that is, to which organizations would your organization give support?

Q24. Which organizations on this list would be likely to come to (your organization's) support in time of trouble?

Fine. Now this final section has some questions about your background. Although they ask about you, keep in mind that they are to be used in a statistical form only, much like the U.S. Census.

Q25. When were you born? (Get year of birth.)

Q26. Was the place in which you mainly grew up a large city of over 50,000; the suburb of such a large city; a small city or town; or a farm?

Q27. What state was that in?

Q28. (If Illinois) In what city?

Q29. About how many years have you lived in Towertown?

Q30. Are you married, single, widowed, divorced, or separated?

Q31. (If not single) How many children do you have?

Q32. Do your parents originate from Towertown or its surrounding area?

Q33. What is your principal occupation at the present time? (Please get exact particulars. If retired or currently unemployed, indicate below and then ask for last main occupation. If respondent has two jobs, determine which is the main one and indicate both.)

Q34. What kind of business is (was) that in? (e.g., steelmill, bank, etc.) (Get name of specific organization also.)

Q35. Do you work for yourself or for someone else?

   Self
   Someone else

   (If "Self") About how many people do you employ?   None
                                                     1-9
                                                     10-24
                                                     25-49
                                                     50-99
                                                     100-499
                                                     500 or more

   (If "Someone else") About how many people are
   employed by the company you work for?   None
                                                     1-9
                                                     10-24
                                                     25-49
                                                     50-99
                                                     100-499
                                                     500 or more

   (If "Someone else") Are you the supervisor of other
   people? (If "yes") How many people are you responsible for?   None
                                                     1-9
                                                     10-24
                                                     25-49
                                                     50-99
                                                     100-499
                                                     500 or more

Q36. What was the principal occupation of your father? (Obtain exact
   particulars.)

Q37. How many years of school did you complete?

   0-8 years
   9-11 years (some high school)
   12 years (high school graduate)
   13-15 years (some college) What college or university?
   16 years (college graduate) What college or university?
   17 or more years (graduate training) What college or university? What
   degree?
   Other (e.g., vocational training)

Q38. Do you have a religious preference? That is, are you either Protestant, Roman Catholic, Jewish, or something else? (Probe on this last item.)

(If "Protestant") What specific denomination?

Q39 About how often, if ever, have you attended religious services in the last year? (Hand Card G with alternatives.)

More than once a week
Once a week
Two or three times a month
Once a month
A few times a year or less
Never

Q40. What nationality background do you think of yourself as having—that is, besides being American? (Accept clear assertion of "Only American" nationality without probe. Always record exact answer.)

Q41. Generally speaking, do you think of yourself a Republican or a Democrat?

(If "Republican" or "Democrat") Would you call yourself a strong (Republican/Democrat) or not a very strong (Republican/Democrat)?

(If "Independent") Do you think of yourself as closer to the Republican or Democratic party?

Q42. What about your father? When you were growing up, was your father more a Republican or more a Democrat?

Q43. We have here once again our list of organizations and voluntary associations in Towertown. (Hand over group list.)

Would you please first tell us the organizations and voluntary associations in which you are a member?

(If no memberships mentioned or respondent belongs to organizations not listed) Are there other organizations or voluntary associations in which you are a member? (Note specific names of organizations.)

(For each organization that a respondent is a member of ask the following questions.) Are you at this time:
     a holder of an executive position in (organization)
     an active member, that is, do you participate frequently in events or meetings of the (organization), or
     only an inactive or paying member?

Q44. Do you presently have an office (including honorary) or are you a member of a committee, or do you have othersie an official (governmental) position in the city or county? (Have respondent give details.)

Q45. Do you presently hold an official governmental position above the county level?

Q46. How about boards of directors or of trustees or similar non-political offices and honorary positions?

Name of respondent:
Address:
Phone:
Interviewer:
Date of interview:
Place:
Duration of interview: (in minutes)
Cooperativeness of respondent:
     Very cooperative and responsive throughout
     Cooperative ("about average")
     Relatively uncooperative and hostile
General remarks:

APPENDIX C:
TELEPHONE QUESTIONNAIRE
FOR ORGANIZATIONAL AGENTS

A. Age
   Q1.   How old is (your organization)?

   _____

   Q2.   How many years has (your organization) been in Towertown?

   _____

B. Personnel
   Q3.   How many people does (your organization) employ in Tower-
          town?

   _____

   Q3a.   (If voluntary association) How many members are there in (your
          organization)?

   _____

   Q4.   How many administrators does (your organization) have?

   _____

   Q4a.   (If voluntary association) How many officers, board members,
          and committeemen does (your organization) have?

   _____

C.   Budget

      Q5.   What is (your organization) annual budget/sales?

               _____

      Q6.   What are (your organization) total budget/sales?

               _____

      Q7.   What percent of (your organization) budget comes from public funds, and what percent comes from private/church funds?

               _____% public

               _____% private/church

      Q8.   What percent of all the money that comes into (your organization) comes from inside the county?

               _____% from inside the county

      Q9.   What percent of all money that goes out from (your organization) stays in the county?

               _____% to this county

D.   Organization Structure

      Q10.   In your opinion, what are the principal activities or tasks of (your organization)?

            a) _____

            b) _____

            c) _____

Now thinking about those individuals who perform those tasks,

      Q11.   What is their average education?

            a) _____

            b) _____

            c) _____

Q12. Is it necessary for them to have at least 6 mos. of specialized training?

a) _____

b) _____

c) _____

Q13. And finally, how much discretion do these individuals have in carrying out their work, i.e., can workers determine how they are to go about doing their work?

a) 1. Never   2. Seldom   3. About half the time   4. Most of the time   5. Always

b) 1. Never   2. Seldom   3. About half the time   4. Most of the time   5. Always

c) 1. Never   2. Seldom   3. About half the time   4. Most of the time   5. Always

Q14. (If voluntary association) What is the average education of (your organization) membership?

_____

E. Organizational Involvement in Issues

Q15. Did or would (your organization) participate in any way in the decision-making process concerning the . . . (check if they did)

a) Construction of the new health center _____

b) Town curfew in the Spring of 1970 _____

c) Location of the new post office _____

d) Program at Garvey School _____

e) Jurisdiction over a new airport _____

If answered "yes" to any of the above issues, ask questions Q16 to Q18 for the issues that his organization became involved in.

Q16. And why did your organization become involved? (read alternatives, respondent can choose more than one)

a) Construction of the new health center

1. Own self interest	2. Concern for larger community	3. Within organizational domain	4. Asked to be involved	5. Personal desire of leaders

b) Town curfew in the Spring of 1970

1. Own self interest	2. Concern for larger community	3. Within organizational domain	4. Asked to be involved	5. Personal desire of leaders

c) Location of the new post office

1. Own self interest	2. Concern for larger community	3. Within organizational domain	4. Asked to be involved	5. Personal desire of leaders

d) Program at Garvey School

1. Own self interest	2. Concern for larger community	3. Within organizational domain	4. Asked to be involved	5. Personal desire of leaders

e) Jurisdiction over a new airport

1. Own self interest	2. Concern for larger community	3. Within organizational domain	4. Asked to be involved	5. Personal desire of leaders

Q17. And what role(s) did (your organization) play in the decision-making process?

a) Construction of the new health center

1. Initiated issue	2. Supported issue	3. Opposed issue	4. Advisor	5. Official decision-maker

b) Town curfew in the Spring of 1970

1. Initiated issue	2. Supported issue	3. Opposed issue	4. Advisor	5. Official decision-maker

c) Location of the new post office

1. Initiated issue	2. Supported issue	3. Opposed issue	4. Advisor	5. Official decision-maker

d) Program at Garvey School

1. Initiated   2. Supported   3. Opposed   4. Advisor   5. Official
   issue   issue   issue   decision-maker

e) Jurisdiction over a new airport

1. Initiated   2. Supported   3. Opposed   4. Advisor   5. Official
   issue   issue   issue   decision-maker

   Q18.   Finally, what year and month did (your organization) first become involved in the issue?

	Month	Year
a) Construction of the new health center	_____	_____
b) Town curfew in the Spring of 1970	_____	_____
c) Location of the new post office	_____	_____
d) Program at Garvey School	_____	_____
e) Jurisdiction over a new airport	_____	_____

APPENDIX D:
SOCIAL VALUE INDICATORS

In Appendices B and C we did not include the value items asked of each of our respondents. We will present these here, since in this appendix we will discuss the construction of our value scales. For the analysis of value homophily among organizational elites we constructed seven scales from 31 value items and the ranking of organizational goals (Appendix A, Q1A to Q1G). In this appendix we will present all the value items, describe how each of the scales was constructed, present their frequency distributions, and review the algorithm used to compute value homophily scores for each pair of organizations using the seven scales.

We asked agents to respond to the following items indicating which statement they agreed with more. Our N for each item is 60.[1]

V1 A) The most important job for government is to make it certain that there are good opportunities for each person to get ahead on his own. (80.0%)
    B) The most important job for the government is to guarantee every person a decent and steady job and standard of living. (18.3%)
    C) Neither. (1.7%)

V2 A) The business community should assume more responsibility for maintaining and improving the quality of life for all Americans rather than confining its attention primarily to improving our material standard of living. (85.0%)
    B) The business community should confine its attention solely to economic matters and let other institutions assume responsibility for taking care of social welfare needs. (15.0%)
    C) Neither. (0.0%)

V3 A) A greater degree of government control over business would result in a weakening of this country's economy. (70.0%)

B) The government should assume greater responsibility for coordinating and planning economic activities and development. (30.0%)

C) Neither. (0.0%)

We next asked respondents a question on labor relations.

V4   In strikes between working people and employers, do you usually side with the workers or with the employers?

A) Workers (23.3%)
B) Employers (61.7%)
C) Neither (1.7%)
D) Depends on the issue (13.3%)
E) Don't know (0.0%)

Finally, respondents were handed a booklet with a set of opinions. We asked them to indicate how much they agreed or disagreed with the following statements.

V5   The protection of consumer interests is best insured by a vigorous competition among sellers rather than by federal government intervention and regulation in behalf of consumers.

Agree			Disagree		
Strongly	Moderately	Weakly	Strongly	Moderately	Weakly
(36.7%)	(31.7%)	(5.0%)	(6.7%)	(16.7%)	(3.3%)

V6   To lead a good life, it is necessary to have socially shared religious beliefs.

Agree			Disagree		
Strongly	Moderately	Weakly	Strongly	Moderately	Weakly
(16.7%)	(15.0%)	(8.3%)	(30.0%)	(20.0%)	(10.0%)

V7   Admitted Communits should be allowed to speak and be heard in this community.

Agree			Disagree		
Strongly	Moderately	Weakly	Strongly	Moderately	Weakly
(41.7%)	(28.3%)	(16.7%)	(8.3%)	(3.3%)	(1.7%)

V8   It is not always wise to plan too far ahead because many things turn out to be a matter of circumstances beyond your control anyhow.

Agree			Disagree		
Strongly	Moderately	Weakly	Strongly	Moderately	Weakly
(5.0%)	(10.0%)	(11.7%)	(43.3%)	(25.0%)	(5.0%)

V9   High social or economic position in America is a pretty good sign of an individual's superior ability or efforts.

Agree			Disagree		
Strongly	Moderately	Weakly	Strongly	Moderately	Weakly
(3.3%)	(13.3%)	(13.3%)	(25.0%)	(40.0%)	(5.0%)

V10 A housewife should not expect her husband to help her in the household when he comes home from a hard day's work.

Agree			Disagree		
Strongly	Moderately	Weakly	Strongly	Moderately	Weakly
(3.3%)	(10.0%)	(8.3%)	(20.0%)	(50.0%)	(8.3%)

V11 Labor unions have become too big for the good of the country.

Agree			Disagree		
Strongly	Moderately	Weakly	Strongly	Moderately	Weakly
(21.7%)	(28.3%)	(18.3%)	(5.0%)	(13.3%)	(13.3%)

V12 A man ought to be guided by what his own experience tells him is right rather than by what any institution, such as the church or government, tells him to do.

Agree			Disagree		
Strongly	Moderately	Weakly	Strongly	Moderately	Weakly
(25.0%)	(21.7%)	(6.7%)	(13.3%)	(20.0%)	(13.3%)

V13 There's too much power concentrated in the hands of a few large companies for the good of the country.

Agree			Disagree		
Strongly	Moderately	Weakly	Strongly	Moderately	Weakly
(18.3%)	(30.0%)	(21.7%)	(8.3%)	(16.7%)	(5.0%)

V14 One of the problems in America today is that too many people have too much concern for leisure time activities and not enough about hard work.

Agree			Disagree		
Strongly	Moderately	Weakly	Strongly	Moderately	Weakly
(13.3%)	(23.3%)	(11.7%)	(8.3%)	(30.0%)	(13.3%)

V15 To cope effectively with the problems facing our society, what is needed is a general strengthening and reliance on local governmental institutions, rather than the federal government, in finding solutions to these problems.

	Agree			Disagree		
	Strongly	Moderately	Weakly	Strongly	Moderately	Weakly
	(31.7%)	(51.7%)	(6.7%)	(0.0%)	(5.0%)	(5.0%)

V16 Differences in rank among people are acceptable since they are chiefly the result of the way individuals have made use of the opportunity open to them.

	Agree			Disagree		
	Strongly	Moderately	Weakly	Strongly	Moderately	Weakly
	(6.7%)	(21.7%)	(25.0%)	(13.3%)	(26.7%)	(6.7%)

V17 A father should share equally with the mother in taking care of the needs of infants and very young children.

	Agree			Disagree		
	Strongly	Moderately	Weakly	Strongly	Moderately	Weakly
	(21.7%)	(30.0%)	(11.7%)	(5.0%)	(21.7%)	(10.0%)

V18 Churches are necessary to establish or preserve concepts of right and wrong.

	Agree			Disagree		
	Strongly	Moderately	Weakly	Strongly	Moderately	Weakly
	(21.7%)	(25.0%)	(23.3%)	(3.3%)	(20.0%)	(6.7%)

V19 Law enforcement officials should have the right to listen in on private telephone conversations whenever in their judgment it is necessary for carrying on their work.

	Agree			Disagree		
	Strongly	Moderately	Weakly	Strongly	Moderately	Weakly
	(1.7%)	(6.7%)	(5.0%)	(66.7%)	(20.0%)	(0.0%)

V20 For the good of the country, many of our largest companies ought to be broken up into smaller companies.

	Agree			Disagree		
	Strongly	Moderately	Weakly	Strongly	Moderately	Weakly
	(3.3%)	(15.0%)	(31.7%)	(15.0%)	(25.0%)	(10.0%)

V21 The right to associate with whom one pleases is being endangered by the excesses of civil rights legislation.

	Agree			Disagree		
	Strongly	Moderately	Weakly	Strongly	Moderately	Weakly
	(8.3%)	(10.0%)	(8.3%)	(33.3%)	(33.3%)	(6.7%)

V22 For all the criticisms one may direct against President Nixon, he was basically correct in his emphasis on leaving Vietnam with our national honor intact.

Agree			Disagree		
Strongly	Moderately	Weakly	Strongly	Moderately	Weakly
(23.3%)	(16.7%)	(21.7%)	(23.3%)	(11.7%)	(3.3%)

V23 The final decision about major financial issues should be made by the man of the house.

Agree			Disagree		
Strongly	Moderately	Weakly	Strongly	Moderately	Weakly
(3.3%)	(11.7%)	(8.3%)	(45.0%)	(26.7%)	(5.0%)

V24 Government authorities should be allowed to ban books and movies which they consider harmful to the public morality.

Agree			Disagree		
Strongly	Moderately	Weakly	Strongly	Moderately	Weakly
(3.3%)	(10.0%)	(8.3%)	(50.0%)	(23.3%)	(5.0%)

V25 Religious education is essential to preserve the morals of our society.

Agree			Disagree		
Strongly	Moderately	Weakly	Strongly	Moderately	Weakly
(13.3%)	(28.3%)	(23.3%)	(10.0%)	(11.7%)	(13.3%)

V26 Most unions try to prevent the efficient use of labor.

Agree			Disagree		
Strongly	Moderately	Weakly	Strongly	Moderately	Weakly
(11.7%)	(11.7%)	(16.7%)	(11.7%)	(28.3%)	(20.0%)

V27 A housewife with children under six years of age should not work.

Agree			Disagree		
Strongly	Moderately	Weakly	Strongly	Moderately	Weakly
(13.3%)	(23.3%)	(18.3%)	(10.0%)	(25.0%)	(10.0%)

V28 There are people in low positions in America because most of them do not want the responsibility of higher positions.

Agree			Disagree		
Strongly	Moderately	Weakly	Strongly	Moderately	Weakly
(6.7%)	(16.7%)	(15.0%)	(20.0%)	(31.7%)	(10.0%)

V29 Economic profits are by and large justly distributed in the United States today.

Agree			Disagree		
Strongly	Moderately	Weakly	Strongly	Moderately	Weakly
(6.7%)	(13.3%)	(20.0%)	(20.0%)	(31.7%)	(8.3%)

V30 The gains that labor unions win for their members help make the country more prosperous.

Agree			Disagree		
Strongly	Moderately	Weakly	Strongly	Moderately	Weakly
(5.0%)	(30.0%)	(31.7%)	(13.3%)	(15.0%)	(5.0%)

V31 Differences in prestige among occupations should be reduced.

Agree			Disagree		
Strongly	Moderately	Weakly	Strongly	Moderately	Weakly
(11.7%)	(36.7%)	(13.3%)	(13.3%)	(8.3%)	(16.7%)

From questions V1 to V31 and Q1A to A16 (Appendix A) we constructed our seven value scales. Below we identify the scale, the items that we used to construct the scale, and the frequency distributions for each scale. The score that a respondent received for a given scale was simply the number of his responses to a subset of questions that were favorable to a given position.[2] The final scale, material community goals, was constructed somewhat differently. From a factor analysis we learned that goals Q1C, Q1D, and Q1G constituted one factor while goals Q1A, Q1B, Q1E, and Q1F formed a second factor, orthogonal to the first. Upon examination of the content of these factors, it was apparent that the first factor tapped an orientation towards "people-oriented" goals, while the second factor tapped an orientation toward "material goals." In computing a scale for "material goals," we assigned a value of "0" if an agent did not mention Q1A, Q1B, Q1E or Q1F as among the three most important goals for a community; a "1" was assigned if an agent mentioned only one of the four goals as among the three most important goals for the community; "2" if two of the four goals were mentioned; and "3" if three of the four goals were mentioned.

GOVECON: Government intervention in the economy

Items	Pro	Con
V1	B	A
V3	B	A
V5	Disagree	Agree

V13		Agree	Disagree
V20		Agree	Disagree
Frequencies	No. of items pro GOVECON	Frequency	Percentage
In favor of gov-	5	2	3.3
ernment	4	10	16.7
intervention	3	6	10.0
	2	18	30.0
	1	13	21.7
Against government	0	11	18.3
intervention		60	100.0

CIVILIB: Civil Liberties

Item		Pro	Con
V7		Agree	Disagree
V19		Disagree	Agree
V21		Disagree	Agree
V24		Disagree	Agree
Frequencies	No. of items pro CIVLIB	Frequency	Percentage
In favor of	4	32	53.3
civil liberties	3	16	26.7
	2	7	11.7
	1	5	8.3
Against civil liberties	0	0	0.0
		60	100.0

RELTRAD: Religious traditionalism

Items		Pro	Con
V6		Agree	Disagree
V18		Agree	Disagree
V25		Agree	Disagree
Frequencies	No. of items pro RELTRAD	Frequency	Percentage
In favor of religious	3	18	30.0
traditionalism	2	16	26.7
	1	19	31.7
Against religious	0	7	11.7
traditionalism		60	100.0

FAMTRAD: Family traditionalism

Items	Pro	Con
V10	Agree	Disagree
V23	Agree	Disagree
V27	Agree	Disagree

Frequencies	No. of items Pro FAMTRAD	Frequency	Percentage
In favor of family traditionalism	3	6	10.0
	2	12	20.0
	1	18	30.0
Against family traditionalism	0	24	40.0
		60	100.0

UNIONS: Unions

Items	Pro A	Con B
V4	Disagree	Agree
V11	Disagree	Agree
V26	Disagree	Disagree
V30	Agree	Disagree

Frequencies	No. of items pro UNIONS	Frequency	Percentage
In favor of unions	4	9	15.0
	3	10	16.7
	2	14	23.3
	1	15	25.0
Against unions	0	12	20.0
		60	100.0

INEQUAL: Social Inequalities

Items	Pro	Con
V9	Agree	Disagree
V16	Agree	Disagree
V28	Agree	Disagree
V29	Agree	Disagree

Frequencies	No. of items pro INEQUAL	Frequency	Percentage

In favor of social	4	5	8.3
inequalities.	3	12	20.0
	2	12	20.0
	1	17	28.3
Against social	0	14	23.3
inequalities.		60	100.0

MATGOALS: Material Community Goals

Items	Pro	Con
Q1A	Chosen as Objective	Not Chosen as Objective
Q1B	Chosen as Objective	Not Chosen as Objective
Q1E	Chosen as Objective	Not Chosen as Objective
Q1F	Chosen as Objective	Not Chosen as Objective

Frequencies	No. of items Pro MATGOALS	Frequency	Percentage
In favor of	3	17	28.3
material goals	2	22	36.7
	1	19	31.7
Against material	0	2	3.3
goals		60	100.0

The computation of value homophily scores for each pair of organizational agents was straightforward once the value scales were constructed. A measure of homophily was computed for each ij pair of agents ($N = n(n-1)/2 = (60(59)/2) = 1770$) using the following algorithm:

$$V_{ij} = \sum_{k=1}^{7} | (S_{ki} - S_{kj}) |$$

where V_{ij} is the score of value homophily for actors i and j, S_{ki} is the score of actor i on the value scale k, and S_{kj} is the score of actor j on the value scale k. We assumed that these scores were estimates of the proximities among organizations regarding social values and submitted them as input to a SSA-1.

NOTES FOR APPENDIX D

1. There were thirteen organizations that we omitted from our analysis of value homophily. First, organizations were omitted if their agent was the spokesperson for

another organization. This eliminated six organizations. We also eliminated the city council because it was impossible to determine which of the seven councilmen was the primary agent. Finally, we dropped six more organizations due to missing data on value items. If we were unable to construct even one of the seven scales for an agent, the agent and its organization were excluded from our analysis.

2. For the sake of simplicity items V5 through V18 were dichotomized so that actors either agreed or disagreed with the statement.

REFERENCES

ADAMEK, R., LAVIN, B. (1975) "Interorganizational exchange: A note on the scarcity hypothesis." Pp. 196-209 in *Interorganization Theory,* edited by A. Negandhi. Kent, Ohio: Kent State University Press.

AIKEN, M., ALFORD, R. (1970) "Community structure and innovation: The case of urban renewal." *American Sociological Review* 35:650-665.

AIKEN, M., HAGE, J. (1968) "Organizational interdependence and intra-organizational structure." *American Sociological Review* 33:912-933.

AIKEN, M., MOTT, P. (1970) *The Structure of Community Power.* New York: Random House.

ALBA, R., KESSLER, R. (1977) "Patterns of interethnic marriage: Persisting ethnic diversity?" Paper presented at the 72nd Annual Meetings of the American Sociological Association, Chicago, September 5-9.

ALDRICH, H. (1975) "An organization-environment perspective on cooperation and conflict between organizations in the manpower training system." Pp. 49-70 in *Interorganization Theory,* edited by A. Negandhi. Kent, Ohio: Kent State University Press.

——— (1976) "Resource dependence and interorganizational relations. Relations between local employment service offices and social services sector organizations." *Administration and Society* 7:419-454.

ALDRICH, H., PFEFFER, J. (1976) "Environments of organizations." Pp. 79-105 in *Annual Review of Sociology* Vol. 2, edited by A. Inkeles. Palo Alto: Annual Reviews Inc.

ALFORD, R. (1975) *Health Care Politics.* Chicago: University of Chicago Press.

ALINSKY, S. (1969) *Rules for Radicals.* Chicago: University of Chicago Press.

ALLEN, M. (1974) "The structure of interorganizational elite cooptation: Interlocking corporate directorates." *American Sociological Review* 39:393-406.

——— (1978) "Economic interest groups and the corporate elite." *Social Science Quarterly* 58:597-615.

APPLEBAUM, R. (1970) *Theories of Social Change.* Chicago: Markham.

ARROW, K. (1955) *Social Choice and Individual Value.* New Haven, Conn.: Yale University Press.

BACHRACH, P., BARATZ, M. (1962) "Two faces of power." *American Political Science Review* 56:947-52.

——— (1963) "Decisions and non-decisions: An analytical framework." *American Political Science Review* 33:912-933.

BANFIELD, E. (1961) *Political Influence.* New York: Free Press.

BARSKY, S. (1974) "Representations of community: Scholars, mass media, and government." Unpublished dissertation, Department of Sociology, University of Chicago.

BARTH, E., JOHNSON, S. (1959) "Community power and a typology of social issues." *Social Forces* 38:29-32.

BAVELAS, A. (1960) "Communication patterns in task oriented groups." Pp. 669-682 in *Group Dynamics: Research and Theory,* edited by D. Cartwright and A. Zander. Evanston, Ill.: Row and Peterson.

BENSON, J.K. (1975) "The interorganizational network as a political economy." *Administrative Science Quarterly* 20:229-49.

——— (1977) "Innovation and crisis in organizational analysis." *Sociological Quarterly* 18:3-16.

BENTLEY, A. (1908) *The Process of Government: A Study of Social Pressures.* Chicago: University of Chicago Press.

BICK, W., MULLER, P. (1978) "Stable patterns within a network of urban bureaucracies." Paper presented at the 73rd Annual Meetings of the American Sociological Association, San Francisco, September 4-8.

BLALOCK, H. (1967) *Toward a Theory of Minority Group Relations.* New York: John Wiley.

BLAU, P. (1964) *Exchange and Power in Social Life.* New York: John Wiley.

——— (1975) "Introduction: Parallels and contrasts in structural inquiries." Pp. 1-20 in *Approaches to the Study of Social Structure,* edited by P. Blau. New York: Free Press.

——— (1977) "A macrosociological theory of social structure." *American Journal of Sociology* 83:26-54.

———, DUNCAN, O.D. (1967) *The American Occupational Structure.* New York: John Wiley.

BOORMAN, S., WHITE, H. (1976) "Social structure from multiple networks. II. Role structures." *American Journal of Sociology* 81:1384-1446.

BREIGER, R., BOORMAN, S., ARABIE, P. (1975) "An algorithm for clustering relational data with applications to social network analysis and comparison with multidimensional scaling." *Journal of Mathematical Psychology* 12:328-383.

BREIGER, R., PATTISON, P. (1978) "The joint role structure of two communities' elites." *Sociological Methods and Research* 7:213-226.

BUCKLEY, W. (1968) *Modern Systems Research for the Behavioral Scientist.* Chicago: Aldine.

BURT, R. (1976) "Positions in networks." *Social Forces* 55:93-122.

——— (1977a) "Positions in multiple network systems, part one: A general conception of stratification and prestige in a system of actors cast as a social topology." *Social Forces* 56:106-131.

——— (1977b) "Power in a social topology." *Social Science Research* 6:1-83.

CARO, R. (1974) *The Power Broker: Robert Moses and the Fall of New York.* New York: Knopf.

CHAPIN, F.S. (1928) *Cultural Change.* New York: Century Co.

CLARK, T. (1968) *Community Structure and Decision-making: Comparative Analyses.* San Francisco: Chandler.

——— (1971) "Community structure and decision-making, budget expenditures, and urban renewal in 51 cities." Pp. 293-313 in *Community Politics: A Behavioral Approach,* edited by C. Bonjean, T. Clark, and R. Lineberry. New York: Free Press.

——— (1972) "The structure of community influence." Pp. 283-314 in *People and Politics in Urban Society*, edited by H. Hahn. Beverly Hills: Sage.

——— (1973a) "Citizen values, power, and policy outputs: A model of community decision-making." *Journal of Comparative Administration* 4:385-427.

——— (1973b) *Community Power and Policy Outputs: A Review of Urban Research.* Beverly Hills: Sage.

——— (1975) "Community power." Pp. 271-296 in *Annual Review of Sociology*, edited by A. Inkeles, J. Coleman, and N. Smelser. Palo Alto, Calif.: Annual Reviews Inc.

COLEMAN, J. (1957) *Community Conflict.* New York: Free Press.

——— (1966) "Foundations for a theory of collective decisions." *American Journal of Sociology* 71:615-627.

——— (1971) *Resources for Social Change: Race in the United States.* New York: Wiley Interscience.

——— (1973a) "Loss of power." *American Sociological Review* 38:1-15.

——— (1973b) *The Mathematics of Collective Action.* Chicago: Aldine.

———, KATZ, E., MENZEL, H. (1966) *Medical Innovation: A Diffusion Study.* Indianapolis: Bobbs-Merrill.

COOK, K. (1977) "Exchange and power in networks of interorganizational relations." *Sociological Quarterly* 18:62-82.

DAHL, R. (1961) *Who Governs? Democracy and Power in an American City.* New Haven, Conn.: Yale University Press.

DAHRENDORF, R. (1958) "Towards a theory of social conflict." *Journal of Conflict Resolution* 11:170-183.

——— (1959) *Class and Class Conflict in Industrial Society.* Stanford: Stanford University Press.

DAVIS, K., MOORE, W. (1945) "Some principles of stratification." *American Sociological Review* 10:242-49.

DEGH, L., VAZSONYI, A. (1975) "The hypothesis of multi-conduit transmission in folklore." Pp. 207-52 in *Folklore: Performance and Communication*, edited by D. Ben-Amos and K. Goldstein. The Hague: Elsevier.

deSWANN, A. (1973) *Coalitions Theories and Cabinet Formation.* The Hague: Elsevier.

DEUTSCH, K. (1963) *The Nerves of Government: Models of Political Communication and Control.* New York: Free Press.

DOWNS, A. (1957) *An Economic Theory of Democracy.* New York: Harper and Row.

EMERSON, R. (1962) "Power dependence relations." *American Sociological Review* 27:31-41.

ETZIONI-HALEVY, E., ETZIONI, A. (1973) *Social Change.* New York: Basic.

EVAN, W. (1966) "The organizational set." Pp. 173-191 in *Approaches to Organizational Design*, edited by J. Thompson. Pittsburgh: University of Pittsburgh Press.

FIELD, A. (1970) *Urban Power Structures: Problems in Theory and Research.* Troy, New York: Schenkman.

FISH, J. (1973) *Black Power/White Control: The Struggle of the Woodlawn Organization in Chicago.* Princeton, N.J.: Princeton University Press.

FORM, W., MILLER, D. (1960) *Industry, Labor, and Community.* New York: Harper and Row.

FREEMAN, L. (1968) *Patterns of Local Community Leadership.* New York: Bobbs-Merrill.

FRENCH, J., RAVEN, B. (1959) "The basis of social power." Pp. 150-67 in *Studies in Social Power*, edited by D. Cartwright. Ann Arbor: Institute for Social Research.

GALASKIEWICZ, J. (1978) "Interest group politics from a comparative perspective."
    Unpublished paper, Department of Sociology, University of Minnesota.
———, BULCROFT, R. (1978) "Metropolitan corporate linkages: A time series analysis."
    Paper presented at the Annual Meetings of the Midwest Sociological Association,
    Omaha, April 12-15.
GALASKIEWICZ, J., MARSDEN, P. (1978) "Interorganizational resource networks:
    Formal patterns of overlap." *Social Science Research* 7:89-107.
GALASKIEWICZ, J., SHATIN, D. (1978) "The social organization of the urban neigh-
    borhood: An application of a network perspective." Paper presented at the Interna-
    tional Network for Social Network Analysis Conference on "New directions in
    structural analysis," Toronto, March 16-18.
GAMSON, W. (1961) "A theory of coalition formation." *American Sociological Review*
    26:373-382.
——— (1966a) "Rancorous conflict in community politics." *American Sociological
    Review* 31:71-80.
——— (1966b) "Reputation and resources in community politics." *American Journal of
    Sociology* 72:121-131.
——— (1968) *Power and Discontent.* Homewood, Ill.: Dorsey.
GOULDNER, A. (1960) "The norm of reciprocity." *American Sociological Review*
    25:161-177.
——— (1970) *The Coming Crisis of Western Sociology.* New York: Basic.
GRANOVETTER, M. (1974) *Getting a Job: A Study of Contacts and Careers.* Cam-
    bridge, Mass.: Harvard University Press.
GRIMES, M., BONJEAN, C., LYON, J., LINEBERRY, R. (1976) "Community structure
    and leadership arrangements: A multidimensional analysis." *American Sociological
    Review* 41:706-725.
GUEST, R. (1962) "Managerial succession in complex organizations." *American Journal
    of Sociology* 68:47-54.
GUETZKOW, H. (1966) "Relations among organizations." Pp. 13-44 in *Studies on
    Behavior in Organizations,* edited by R. Bowers. Athens, Ga.: University of Georgia
    Press.
GUTTMAN, L. (1968) "A general nonmetric technique for finding the smallest coordi-
    nate space for a configuration of points." *Psychometrika* 33:469-506.
HAGE, J., DEWAR, R. (1973) "Elite values versus organizational structure in predicting
    innovation." *Administrative Science Quarterly* 18:279-290.
HALL, R. (1972) *Organizations: Structure and Process.* Englewood Cliffs, N.J.: Prentice-
    Hall.
———, CLARK, J. (1975) "Problems in the study of interorganizational relationships."
    Pp. 111-27 in *Interorganization Theory,* edited by A. Negandhi. Kent, Ohio: Kent
    State University Press.
———, GIORDANO, P., JOHNSON, P., VanROEKEL, M. (1977) "Patterns of interorga-
    nizational relationships." *Administrative Science Quarterly* 22:457-474.
HANNAN, M., FREEMAN, J. (1977) "The population ecology of organizations."
    American Journal of Sociology 82:929-64.
HARARY, F., NORMAN, R., CARTWRIGHT, D. (1965) *Structural Models: An Intro-
    duction to the Theory of Directed Graphs.* New York: John Wiley.
HAWLEY, A. (1951) *Human Ecology: A Theory of Community Structure.* New York:
    Ronald.
——— (1963) "Community power and urban renewal success." *American Journal of
    Sociology* 68:422-31.

HAYES, E. (1972) *Power Structure and Urban Policy: Who Rules in Oakland?* New York: McGraw-Hill.

HERNES, G. (1976) "Structural change in social processes." *American Journal of Sociology* 82:513-547.

HOLLAND, P., LEINHARDT, S. (1977) "A dynamic model for social networks," *Journal of Mathematical Sociology* 5:5-20.

——— (1978) "Social structure as a network process." *Zeitschrift fur Soziologie* 6:386-402.

HOMANS, G. (1958) "Social behavior as exchange." *American Journal of Sociology* 62:597-606.

HUNTER, F. (1953) *Community Power Structure: A Study of Decision Makers.* Chapel Hill: University of North Carolina Press.

KELLER, S. (1963) *Beyond the Ruling Class: Strategic Elites in Modern Society.* New York: Random House.

KASARDA, J., JANOWITZ, M. (1974) "Community attachment in mass society." *American Sociological Review* 39:328-339.

KATZ, D., KAHN, R. (1966) *Social Psychology of Organizations.* New York: John Wiley.

KAUFMAN, H. (1959) "Toward an interaction conception of community." *Social Forces* 38:8-17.

KLONGLAN, G., WARREN, R., WINKELPLECK, J., PAULSON, S. (1976) "Interorganizational measurement in the social service sector: Differences by hierarchical level." *Administrative Science Quarterly* 21:675-87.

KNOKE, D., ROGERS, D. (1978) "A Blockmodel analysis of interorganizational networks." Paper presented at the 73rd Annual Meetings of the American Sociological Association, San Francisco, September 4-8.

KORNBLUM, W. (1974) *Blue Collar Community.* Chicago: University of Chicago Press.

LASSWELL, H. (1950) *Politics: Who Gets What, When, and How.* New York: Peter Smith.

LAUMANN, E.O. (1966) *Prestige and Association in an Urban Community: An Analysis of an Urban Stratification System.* Indianapolis: Bobbs-Merrill.

——— (1973) *Bonds of Pluralism: The Form and Substance of Urban Social Networks.* New York: Wiley Interscience.

———, GALASKIEWICZ, J., MARSDEN, P. (1978) "Community structure as interorganizational linkages." Pp. 455-484 in *Annual Review of Sociology* Vol. 4, edited by R. Turner, J. Coleman, and R. Fox. New York: Annual Reviews Inc.

LAUMANN, E.O., GUTTMAN, L. (1966) "The relative associational contiguity of occupations in an urban setting." *American Sociological Review* 31: 169-78.

LAUMANN, E.O., HOUSE, J. (1970) "Living room styles and social attributes: The patterning of material artifacts in a modern urban community." *Sociology and Social Research* 54:321-342.

LAUMANN, E.O., MARSDEN, P., GALASKIEWICZ, J. (1977) "Community influence structures: Replication and extension of a network approach." *American Journal of Sociology* 83:594-631.

LAUMANN, E.O., PAPPI, F. (1976) *Networks of Collective Action: A Perspective on Community Influence Systems.* New York: Academic Press.

LAWRENCE, P., LORSCH, J. (1967) *Organization and Environment: Managing Differentiation and Integration.* Boston: Division of Research, Graduate School of Business Administration, Harvard University.

LEINHARDT, S. (1977) *Social Networks: A Developing Paradigm*. New York: Academic Press.
LEVINE, J. (1972) "The sphere of influence." *American Sociological Review* 37:14-27.
LEVINE, S., WHITE, P. 1961. "Exchange as a conceptual framework for the study of interorganizational relationships." Administrative Science Quarterly 5:583-601.
———, PAUL, B. (1963) "Community interorganizational problems in providing medical care and social services." *American Journal of Public Health* 53:1183-95.
LEVY, F., MELTSNER, A., WILDAVSKY, A. (1974) *Urban Outcomes: Schools, Streets, and Libraries*. Berkeley: University of California Press.
LIEBERSON, S., O'CONNOR, J. (1972) "Leadership and organizational performance: A study of large corporations." *American Sociological Review* 37:117-130.
LIEBERT, R. (1976) *Disintegration and Political Action: The Changing Functions of City Governments in America*. New York: Academic Press.
LINCOLN, J. (1976) "Power mobilization in the urban community: Reconsidering the ecological approach." *American Sociological Review* 41:1-15.
——— (1977) "Organizational dominance and community structure." Pp. 19-50 in *Power, Paradigms, and Community Research* edited by R. Liebert and A.W. Imershein. Beverly Hills: Sage.
LINGOES, J. (1973) *The Guttman-Lingoes Nonmetric Program Series*. Ann Arbor, Mich.: Mathesis Press.
LITWAK, E., HYLTON, L. (1962) "Interorganizational analysis: A hypothesis of coordinating agencies." *Administrative Science Quarterly* 6:395-421.
LORRAIN, F., WHITE, H. (1971) "Structural equivalence of individuals in social networks." *Journal of Mathematical Sociology* 1:49-80.
LUCE, R.D., RAIFFA, H. (1957) *Games and Decisions*. New York: John Wiley.
LYND, R., LYND, H. (1929) *Middletown*. New York: Harcourt, Brace.
MARRETT, C. (1971) "On the specifications of interorganizational dimensions." *Sociology and Social Research* 56:83-99.
MARSDEN, P., LAUMANN, E.O. (1977) "Collective action in a community elite: Exchange, influence resources, and issue resolution." Pp. 199-250 in *Power, Paradigms, and Community Research*, edited by R. Liebert and A. Imershein. Beverly Hills: Sage.
MARTINDALE, D. (1962) *Social Life and Cultural Change*. Princeton, N.J.: Van Nostrand.
——— (1965) *Functionalism in the Social Sciences: The Strength and Limits of Functionalism in Anthropology, Economics, Political Science, and Sociology*. Philadelphia: American Academy of Political and Social Science.
McFARLAND, D., BROWN, D. (1973) "Social distance as a metric: A systematic introduction to smallest space analysis." Pp. 213-253 in *Bonds of Pluralism: The Form and Substance of Urban Social Networks*, by E.O. Laumann. New York: Wiley Interscience.
MERTON, R.K. (1957a) "The role set: Problems in sociological theory." *British Journal of Sociology* 8:106-20.
——— (1957b) *Social Theory and Social Structure*. Glencoe, Ill.: Free Press.
MICHELS, R. (1949) *Political Parties: A Sociological Study of the Oligarchical Tendencies of Modern Democracy*. Glencoe, Ill.: Free Press.
MILLS, C.W. (1956) *The Power Elite*. New York: Oxford University Press.
MINTZ, B. (1978) "The role of financial institutions in interlock networks." Paper

presented at the International Network for Social Network Analysis Conference on "New directions in structural analysis," Toronto, March 16-18.

MITCHELL, C. (1969) "The concept and use of social networks." Pp. 1-50 in *Social Networks in Urban Situations*, edited by C. Mitchell. Manchester, England: Manchester University Press.

MOLOTCH, H. (1972) *Managed Integration: Dilemmas of Doing Good in the City*. Berkeley: University of California Press.

––– (1976) "The city as a growth machine: Toward a political economy of place." *American Journal of Sociology* 82:309-332.

MOORE, W. (1963) *Social Change*. Englewood Cliffs, N.J.: Prentice-Hall.

MORENO, J. (1953) *Who Shall Survive? Foundations of Sociometry: Group Psychotherapy and Sociodrama*. Boston: Beacon.

MORTIMER, J. (1974) "Patterns of intergenerational occupational movements: A smallest space analysis." *American Journal of Sociology* 79:1278-1299.

MOTT, P. (1970) "The role of the absentee owned corporation in the changing community." Pp. 170-180 in *The Structure of Community Power*, edited by M. Aiken and P. Mott. New York: Random House.

NADEL, S.F. (1957) *The Theory of Social Structure*. London: Cohen and West.

NEGANDHI, A. (1975) *Interorganization Theory*. Kent, Ohio: Kent State University Press.

NIEMI, R., WEISBERG, H. (1972) *Probability Models of Collective Decision-Making*. Columbus, Ohio: Bobs-Merrill.

OLSON, M. (1965) *The Logic of Collective Action: Public Goods and the Theory of Groups*. Cambridge, Mass.: Harvard University Press.

PARSONS, T. (1951) *The Social System*. New York: Free Press.

––– (1956) "Suggestions for a sociological approach to the theory of organizations." *Administrative Science Quarterly* 1:63-69, 74-80.

––– (1963) "On the concept of political power." Proceedings of the American Philosophical Society, 107:232-263.

––– (1966) *Societies: Evolutionary and Comparative Perspective*. Englewood Cliffs, N.J.: Prentice-Hall.

–––, SMELSER, N. (1956) *Economy and Society: A Study in the Integration of Economic and Social Theory*. New York: Free Press.

PERROW, C. (1970) *Organizational Analysis: A Sociological View*. Belmont, Calif.: Wadsworth.

PERRUCCI, R., PILISUK, M. (1970) "Leaders and ruling elites: The interorganizational bases of community power." *American Sociological Review* 35:1040-57.

PFEFFER, J. (1972) "Size and composition of corporate boards of directors: The organization and its environment." *Administrative Science Quarterly* 17:218-228.

POLSBY, N. (1963) *Community Power and Political Theory*. New Haven, Conn.: Yale University Press.

RAKOVE, M. (1976) *Don't Make No Waves . . . Don't Back No Losers*. Bloomington: Indiana University Press.

REID, W. (1964) "Interagency coordination in delinquency prevention and control." *Social Service Review* 38:418-428.

––– (1969) "Interorganizational coordination in social welfare: A theoretical approach to analysis and interpretation." Pp. 176-188 in *Readings in Community Organization Practice*, edited by R. Kramer. Englewood Cliffs, N.J.: Prentice-Hall.

RIKER, W. (1962) *The Theory of Political Coalitions*. New Haven, Conn.: Yale University Press.

ROGERS, D. (1974) "Sociometric analysis of interorganizational relations: Application of theory and measurement." *Rural Sociology* 39:487-503.

ROSE, A. (1967) *The Power Structure: Political Process in American Society.* New York: Oxford, University Press.

ROSKAM, E., LINGOES, J. (1970) "MINISSA-I: A FORTRAN-IV(G) program for the smallest space analysis of square symmetric matrices." *Behavioral Science* 15:204-205.

ROSSI, P., DENTLER, R. (1961) *The Politics of Urban Renewal: The Chicago Findings.* New York: Free Press.

SCAMMON, R. (1958) *America Votes: A Handbook of Contemporary American Election Statistics.* New York: Macmillan.

——— (1972) *America Votes: A Handbook of Contemporary American Election Statistics.* New York: Macmillan.

SCHATTSCHNEIDER, E. (1960) *The Semisovereign People: A Realist's View of Democracy in America.* New York: Holt, Rinehart, and Winston.

SCHULZE, J. (1961) "The bifurcation of power in a satellite city." Pp. 19-80 in *Community Political Systems,* edited by M. Janowitz. New York: Free Press.

SELZNICK, P. (1957) *Leadership in Administration: A Sociological Interpretation.* Evanston, Ill.: Harper, Row, and Peterson.

SHILS, E. (1975) *Center and Periphery.* Chicago: University of Chicago Press.

SMITH, R. (1976) "Community power and decision-making: A replication and extension of Hawley." *American Sociological Review* 41:691-705.

SPERGEL, I. (1976) "Interaction between community structure, delinquency, and social policy in the inner city." Pp. 55-100 in *The Juvenile Justice System,* edited by M. Klein. Beverly Hills: Sage.

SRINIVAS, M.M., BETEILLE, A. (1964) "Networks in Indian social structure." *Man* 64:165-68.

STINCHCOMBE, A. (1968) *Constructing Social Theories.* New York: Harcourt, Brace, and World.

——— (1975) "Merton's theory of social structure." Pp. 11-33 in *The Idea of Social Structure: Papers in Honor of Robert K. Merton,* edited by Lewis Coser. New York: Harcourt, Brace, and Jovanovich.

SUTTLES, G. (1972) *The Social Construction of Communities.* Chicago: University of Chicago Press.

TARAKI, B., WESTBY, D. (1976) "Interorganizational relations: A Comparison of Western and Maoist approaches." Paper presented at the 71st Annual Meetings of the American Sociological Association, New York, September 6-10.

THOMPSON, J. (1967) *Organizations in Action.* New York: McGraw-Hill.

THOMPSON, J., McEWEN, W. (1958) "Organizational goals and environment: Goal-setting as an interaction process." *American Sociological Review* 23:23-31.

TRUMAN, D. (1951) *The Governmental Process: Political Interests and Public Opinion.* New York: Knopf.

TURK, H. (1969) "Comparative urban studies in interorganizational relations." *Sociological Inquiry* 38:108-110.

——— (1970) "Interorganizational networks in urban society: Initial perspectives and comparative research." *American Sociological Review* 35:1-18.

——— (1973a) *Interorganizational Activation in Urban Communities: Deductions from the Concept of System.* Washington, D.C.: Arnold and Caroline Rose Monograph Series, American Sociological Association.

——— (1973b) "Comparative urban structure from an interorganizational perspective." *Administrative Science Quarterly* 18:37-55.

——— (1977) *Organizations in Modern Life: Cities and Other Large Networks.* San Francisco: Jossey-Bass.

VAN de VEN, A., EMMETT, D., KOENIG, R. (1975) "Frameworks for interorganizational analysis." Pp. 19-38 in *Interorganization Theory,* edited by A. Negandhi. Kent, Ohio: Kent State University Press.

von NEUMANN, J., MORGENSTERN, O. (1947) *Theory of Games and Economic Behavior.* Princeton, N.J.: Princeton University Press.

WALTON, J. (1967) "The vertical axis of community organization and the structure of power." *Social Science Quarterly* 48:353-368.

WARREN, R. (1956) "Toward a reformulation of community theory." *Human Organization* 15:8-11.

WARREN, R. (1963) *The Community in America.* Chicago: Rand-McNally.

——— (1967) "The interorganizational field as a focus for investigation." *Administrative Science Quarterly* 12:396-419.

——— (1971) "The sociology of knowledge and the problems of the inner cities." *Social Science Quarterly* 52:469-491.

———, ROSE, S., BERGUNDER, A. (1974) *The Structure of Urban Reform.* Lexington, Mass.: Lexington Books.

WASSERMAN, S. (1977) "Stochastic models for directed graphs." Ph.D. dissertation, Department of Statistics, Harvard University.

WEBER, M. (1947) *The Theory of Social and Economic Organization.* New York: Free Press.

WHITE, H., BOORMAN, S., BREIGER, R. (1976) "Social structure from multiple networks. I. Blockmodels of roles and positions." *American Journal of Sociology* 81:730-80.

WHITE, P. (1974) "Intra- and inter-organizational studies: Do they require separate conceptualizations?" *Administration and Society* 6:107-152.

WILSON, W. (1973) *Power, Racism, and Privilege.* New York: Macmillan.

YUCHTMAN, E., SEASHORE, S. (1967) "A systems resource approach to organizational effectiveness." *American Sociological Review* 32:891-903.

ZALD, M. (1967) "Urban differentiation, characteristics of boards of directors, and organizational effectiveness." *American Journal of Sociology* 73:261-272.

———, BERGER, M. (1978) "Social movements within organizations: Coup d'etat, insurgency, and mass movements." *American Journal of Sociology* 83:823-861.

ZEITLIN, M. (1974) "Corporate ownership and control: The large corporation and the capitalist class." *American Journal of Sociology* 79:1073-1119.

ABOUT THE AUTHOR

JOSEPH GALASKIEWICZ is an assistant professor in the Department of Sociology, University of Minnesota (Twin Cities). He received his Ph.D. in sociology from the University of Chicago in 1976. His most recent research develops many of the themes introduced in this book. He is currently working on a series of papers which examine the linkages between Twin Cities cultural organizations and various actors in their task environment. Special attention is given to the interorganizational linkages between cultural institutions and Minneapolis-St. Paul corporations. He is also writing a monograph with Edward O. Laumann and Peter V. Marsden on interorganizational networks in a second Illinois community. In addition, Professor Galaskiewicz has published several papers on the methodology of doing interorganizational network studies.